LOVE IS BLIND
AND DANGEROUS

LOVE IS BLIND
AND DANGEROUS

▼

The Psychopathic Stalker

A true story by
Brad Dunaway

Writers Club Press
San Jose New York Lincoln Shanghai

LOVE IS BLIND AND DANGEROUS
The Psychopathic Stalker

Writers Club Press
an imprint of iUniverse.com, Inc.

For information address:
iUniverse.com, Inc.
5220 S 16th, Ste. 200
Lincoln, NE 68512
www.iuniverse.com

ISBN: 0-595-19028-6

Printed in the United States of America

CONTENTS

▼

FOREWORD

▼

This true story exposes one of the most frightening social problems in our lives today. Dr. Robert Hare, world-renowned expert on psychopaths, warns us that there are three to four million of them among us. "Sooner or later, everyone will encounter a psychopath." These are not the obviously deranged "psychos" who shoot people or wind up in mental hospitals. Instead, they are the ones who live in our midst and appear normal.

This book is a fascinating journey into the mind of a typical psychopath, well-identified by Robert Hare's Psychopathy Summary Checklist presented herein. The ever-dangerous Marlene, subject of this story, is a real person. All of her activities have been either documented in the public record, or accounted for in privately-held records. For hearsay evidence, two or more persons have offered separate accounts. Although personal names have been changed for protective purposes, no element of this true story has been stretched or invented.

This is a wake-up call for all who fall into the labyrinth of LOVE, an intangible, convoluted emotion: The wonderful stuff which is said to make the world go 'round.

No one explains how vulnerable we are when this emotion takes hold. And, most certainly, no one suggests that a number of suicides and accidents may actually be disguised murders, some of which are carefully and methodically planned. No one advises us to hone our awareness and skepticism skills before entering into a meaningful relationship, just in case that relationship may prove fatal.

"Real life is so amazing," wrote Robert Fulghum. Some stories are stranger than fiction and this, indeed, is one: a narrative that explores ground-breaking insights into the strange world of deception. May this book serve as a beacon for others who become blinded by predators of con artistry and by passions of love.

Palm Springs, California, 2001

SALUDS AND KUDOS

▼

Most of the contributors to this book must remain anonymous, including medical specialists, genealogists, many informants and interviewees. Nevertheless, I am most appreciative of their significant contributions.

The comprehensiveness of this story would not have been possible without the services of "Warren Stellar," *P.I. extraordinaire* whose devotion and brilliance, together with the assistance of his staff, brought a vast amount of information to light. Nor would Marlene's past in Germany, Canada and the midwestern United States have been brought to light so fully without the dedication and devotion of my remarkable wife who served as my chief German/French interpreter.

David Mehnert's skillful editing has been invaluable. I am pleased and proud to have the assistance of this co-author of the award-winning *Citizen Jane*.

I acknowledge the cooperative assistance of a sheriff, attorneys, security guards, secretaries and my close personal friends. *The Desert Sun* and *Palm Springs Life* kindly supplied background materials.

Palm Springs, California, 2001.

CHAPTER I

────────▼────────

IN THE SOUP

"I just found my fiancé in his bathroom asleep on the toilet."

The terse call, as taped by 9-1-1, contains no emotion. There is no concern, no fear, no anxiety.

"Your fiancé is asleep?"

"Yes," replied the woman. "Asleep."

"Do you need help? An ambulance?"

"Yes."

Much later, the dispatcher commented on the bizarre nature of the 9-1-1 call.

March 13, 1993 was a warm, sunny Saturday in Palm Springs. Some remember the lively Saint Patrick's Day party held that evening at Davnet Duggan's home in an exclusive Palm Desert gated community. Others remember the late afternoon commotion of fire trucks, Sheriff, security cars, and ambulance within the prestigious confines of PGA West.

Ten hours after the 9-1-1 call, I, Brad Dunaway, woke up in a strange bed, wondering where I was and how I got there. After surveying the large ward of drab beds in an antiseptic atmosphere, it was obvious I was in a hospital. But which one? The wall clock read 1:00. Was it A.M. or P.M.? It appeared to be nighttime. As the mental fog began to clear, I desperately tried to remember recent events.

Regaining orientation was difficult. What had happened at the Saint Patrick's Day party on Saturday night? Did I go? I didn't drink, smoke or use drugs. "I must not have gone to the party," I thought. "Would Marlene have gone alone? More importantly, what happened to me?"

About 1:30 A.M., I called across the room to the nurse seated at the desk. When she approached, I asked, "What hospital is this?"

"You're in Desert Springs Hospital. You've been in the Emergency Center until a short while ago. How are you feeling?"

"Confused. Why am I here?"

"You may have had a small stroke, but the CAT scan was clear, and your heart is good."

"How odd," I thought. If I didn't have a heart attack or a significant stroke, how could this have happened?

My mind wandered back to the previous day, which was gradually coming into focus. That Saturday morning, my fiancée, Marlene, had asked me to meet her by the lake at the polo grounds where she was going to be horseback riding.

"I'd like you to take pictures of me and my horse, Queen," she said. "You haven't been out there, so I'm writing these directions for you. Should take you only 15 minutes. If you leave at 9:45 A.M. you ought to be there by 10:00 A.M. I'll expect you then."

I was delighted to be invited out to her "retreat," if only to take pictures. Marlene had a habit of riding most Friday and Saturday mornings.

The drive to the lake was uneventful. Perfect directions—but that's Marlene—always very precise and punctual. I anticipated the photo shoot, not that saddle horses were my favorite subject, but Marlene certainly was. Her beauty was superior to any desert scene around her.

I arrived on schedule, but could not find her. Carefully, I checked the written instructions and reviewed them, first with a polo player and then with a clubhouse attendant. Both men pointed out that my car, at the edge of the uncrowded one-acre lake, would be clearly visible to anyone on the riding trail. This, indeed, was the right location, unobstructed by trees and next to the antique car display on the polo grounds.

An hour passed. Marlene never appeared.

Disappointed and perplexed, I decided to run an errand and pick up some golf tournament tickets. By that time, Marlene should be home. However, when I arrived, Marlene was not there. She returned a little past noon, still in her riding togs.

"Sweetie," I said, "I've been worried about you. What happened? I'm sure I followed your directions."

I asked where she had been, because I was certain I had the correct location on the small lake. Normally, Marlene would have had a very direct response, but this time she lightly dismissed the matter.

"I was there. How about your usual soup and sandwich?"

"Fine," I replied, quite puzzled. I didn't want to press the subject, especially with the Saint Patrick's Day party coming up that night. She seemed a bit tentative and tense.

Marlene popped some soup into the microwave as I seated myself at the table in the kitchen alcove, my back to her. She asked about my other activities during the morning. I then asked, "What time is the Saint Patrick's Day Party tonight?" We had been invited to the party at the home of Marlene's best friend, Davnet Duggan.

Marlene had seemed reluctant to go to the party, or even to talk about it, since the invitation arrived. It wasn't inscribed solely to her as she had expected, but to both of us.

As lunch was served, I asked, "What potluck dish are you taking to Davnet's?" She changed the subject. Then I suggested, "On our way to the party we'll be able to listen to Garrison Keillor. He's on the radio between 6:00 and 7:00 P.M." She was less than enthusiastic, even though Keillor was her favorite humorist.

After lunch, Marlene said, "I'm not feeling well. I'm going to take a nap."

"All right," I replied. Such complaints were not unusual lately.

I walked down the long hallway to the corridor that leads in one direction to the master bedroom, where Marlene would lie down, and turned in the other direction to the bedroom that I used to read and nap.

"Are you going to take a nap, too?" asked Marlene in her soft velvety voice, as she headed toward the master bedroom.

"I may." At the moment I was not tired.

"I'll see you about 4:00 P.M. for your favorite treatment," she added as we parted. I liked that. Her lovemaking was magical.

"Wonderful," I responded.

I looked at the morning newspapers briefly, then selected my clothes for the evening, choosing a favorite golf sweater, a recent gift from Marlene. Then I decided to go to my desk in the study. Soon thereafter, I recalled having to go to the bathroom. That was my last conscious thought of the day.

*   *   *

After regaining consciousness and becoming more oriented, I learned that a 9-1-1 call had been made and the ambulance had reached the hospital at 5:15 P.M.

I'd been in the Emergency Center until 9:10 P.M., then was transferred to Intensive Care. With my mind now racing, there was no way I could sleep. I wanted out of the hospital and was determined to get home by any means possible.

At 5:00 A.M. I asked a nurse to phone and request that Marlene hurry to pick me up and bring my clothes. Marlene usually arose at 5:00 A.M.

on Sundays, because she reported to work early at the resort where she was a bookkeeper.

I watched the nurse make the phone call at her desk close to my bed. From her response, I could detect Marlene's dismay that I could sign out and release myself. Marlene seemed aware that the hospital had a general policy of keeping emergency and trauma patients for several days of observation. Her reaction bothered me, as did my discovery that she had not stayed with me overnight.

Of even greater concern was that she had failed to phone all night.

When Marlene didn't arrive by 7:00 A.M., I asked the nurse to phone again. Marlene told the nurse that she had been ill during the night and had fallen back asleep after the 5:00 A.M. call. The hospital would not allow me to take a taxi, nor would it supply street apparel. Marlene had taken my personal effects, including valuables.

A nightmare scenario was slowly dawning on me. Was it my imagination, or was there truly something suspicious about Marlene's actions? What had happened at the polo grounds, and why had I been asked to come photograph her, only to find that she was missing? When she had come home, her jodhpur riding togs were fresh and there was no aroma of leather or horse sweat. She had behaved so mysteriously.

I asked the doctor making the 7:00 A.M. rounds to quantify any drug elements in my urine and blood samples. He told me that only a broad toxic screen had been ordered by the earlier physician on emergency call Saturday night, but added that he would have a full chemical analysis made of the same samples. I made certain the doctor knew I was now concerned about the possibility of Marlene having deliberately drugged me. And I desperately hoped this suspicion would prove to be unfounded.

My anxiety increased with each passing minute. Where was Marlene? I felt alone, much as I'd felt after having my 16-year-old dog, Candy, put to sleep recently. Thinking of Candy's life-size statue now standing in my courtyard brought tears to my eyes. How I missed her! Minutes later, with my mind in fast-forward, I almost chuckled aloud when I thought about someone putting a life-size statue of me in my courtyard after this weekend's incident.

Here I was, a respected career man, divorced in 1988 at the time of my retirement. I was 64 years old, a family man with devoted children. It wasn't mad adventure I was seeking. I wanted to spend my active retirement years with a warm, affectionate woman who would share my interests in a stable and normal relationship with marital affinity. For the past nine months Marlene and I had been engaged, and had been living together in complete serenity.

*   *   *

At 8:00 A.M. Marlene zipped up to the front door of the hospital in her white sports car. My clothes were sent upstairs to me in a sack.

"Just drive," I gruffly requested upon entering the car.

"What's the matter? I called 9-1-1 for you after I found you in the bathroom."

"I'm upset that it took you three hours to get here."

No further conversation took place on the way home. My first concern was getting home in order to find answers to some important questions. I began my own detective work, hoping to find Marlene innocent. After all, she was the woman of my dreams. Marlene was to be my lifelong companion.

CHAPTER 2

▼

BRAD—THE TARGET

I met Marlene in November of 1989, after she responded to a singles ad I had placed in the *Los Angeles Times*. This method of meeting people was then a very popular and reputable way to find a new companion or possible mate, especially in this quiet desert resort area.

My retirement was an exciting time for me. I wanted to take all the turn-outs, smell all the flowers. In my *Los Angeles Times* ad, I wrote that I was looking for a pretty lady, 50-ish, talented, intelligent, and financially independent. I said I enjoyed travel, sports, theater, dancing and nature, and hoped to find someone with similar interests. Although I did not state it in the ad, my ideal was a reliable, caring and romantic woman, supportive and not domineering.

Marlene wrote a letter that was thoughtful, even demure. Her interests harmonized with my own. After speaking with her by phone, I decided to meet Marlene for lunch.

Any doubts I had were dispelled on meeting her in person. I was struck both by Marlene's beauty and by her charm and easygoing humor. A self-confessed workaholic, Marlene had impeccable credentials. She worked as an accountant for Dr. William Randolph, a prominent society dentist in Palm Desert, and performed additional work for Wallace Weller, a Los Angeles-based philanthropist familiar to me both by name and reputation.

This was obviously a woman who enjoyed positions of great trust. To top it off, in her spare time Marlene donated services to the Braille Institute. This was not a woman who could steal someone blind, not in a thousand years.

Marlene was worldly and well-spoken. German by birth, she had emigrated to Canada when she was 15 years old. I was particularly impressed that there was absolutely no hint of an accent in her speech; she had managed to erase all traces of her foreign birth. I could hardly believe that Marlene had an 18-year-old son. She simply looked too young.

I immediately sensed that she would make an excellent travel companion. Her conversation was stimulating, and by the time we had dinner a few days later, bells were ringing for me. Her winsome smile and shapely figure had etched themselves in my mind. Marlene was a find.

*   *   *

I retired as Founder and Chairman Emeritus of a technical firm that had grown into an extremely successful and respected California enterprise. Shortly after retiring in 1988, I divorced Lucille, ending a rocky marriage of a little over ten years, a decade punctuated by numerous separations. She and I had reached an amicable agreement and remained friends.

In truth, my life's longest love had been Linda Dunaway, my first wife of 25 years, a pretty brunette, the mother of my four children. With Linda it was a case of 23 years of good marriage and two years of a deteriorating relationship, unrelated to infidelity. Despite the traumatic divorce, we remained friends. I thought so much of Linda that, when asked before my high school reunion in 1992 what memory I treasured most from my school days, I wrote:

"Meeting Linda on the front steps of the high school for the first time, an event captured and memorialized by a candid photograph that appeared in the high school annual that year."

My retirement stimulated the move to the desert, where most of my time was spent authoring two books, traveling, and playing golf. At 5'10", 175 pounds and with an athletic background, I was in robust health. This was my first real opportunity to enjoy leisure time, and I reveled in meeting new people, especially single women.

Response to my newspaper ad was overwhelming, but I managed to be methodical in the selection process. It seemed easy to weed out the less desirable applicants. Before meeting Marlene, I had already dated several respondents and had met at least 15 of them for lunch.

Dating, however, had not slowed down my travel calendar. High on the priority list were visits to my children and grandchildren, and I took 15 or more out-of-state trips in 1989 alone. In December 1989 I attended a Bowl game in Florida, and took the opportunity to visit my ex-wife, Lucille, and her mother. They were wintering in Lucille's luxurious RV. Without going into details, I told Lucille that I had been dating again. For her part, Lucille let me know that she had not informed her mother of our divorce because of her mother's heart condition.

In January 1990, I took Marlene to the Bob Hope Festival Ball, a premiere charity event. This was the start of her becoming my Cinderella at many balls. The two of us had so much in common. We laughed together, and appreciated the importance of a sense of humor. We liked the same health foods and didn't smoke or drink. While she rode horseback, I swam or golfed. Marlene often caddied for me on trips, no easy task with this golfer's zigzag path from tee to green.

I admired her ear for music and her eye for paintings. She expressed a preference for classical or jazz, as well as romantic ballads. Among her favorite ballads were those by Julio Iglesias, especially those sung in German. She seemed to like the Romanticism and Impressionist schools of art, with bright settings and scenes.

Later in January we traveled to the Big Island of Hawaii for the Senior Skins golf matches. Our whimsical antics seemed to reach new heights. Marlene posed in front of the "SKINS GAME" entrance sign, fleetingly exposing her topless beauty. We laughed at the difference between the Skins Game played on this golf course, and our favorite "skins game" played in privacy. This was but one of many joyful moments on this trip. When we returned home, I stopped seeing other women, believing that I was in love with Marlene.

Casa del Vista was the lodestar of our romance. A spacious and rambling estate, Casa del Vista is a small desert oasis in the private community of PGA West. Adjoining the red-tiled hacienda is a walled Spanish courtyard containing a swimming pool, spa, fountain and gazebo. The gorgeous bougainvillea vines on the walls and porticos shed their pink petals in the desert breeze, seducing every first-time visitor to Casa del Vista. My favorite refuge, however, is the rose garden, which blooms year round and smells of heady perfume. I am reminded that the word "paradise" comes from an old Persian word meaning "walled garden." Casa del Vista is indeed such a place.

Like many women in the desert, Marlene was attracted by the designer fashion and art shows, and concerts such as the Orchester der Beethovenhalle Bonn. Annual tennis and golf tournaments were of interest, especially the Bob Hope Classic.

It wasn't long before Marlene would stay overnight, and then several days at a time. What was this magic elixir that compelled us to consume each other? After gentle foreplay, she'd flatten her ample breasts against my chest as our toes and hands intertwined. Her pleasure was verbalized at every stroke of her silken body. We drew each other closer, twisting and turning as one. Our bodies thrilled to each other's touch as our ignited movements synchronized with the soft stereo music. Each day of our whirlwind romance seemed to unite us, buoyed by the greatest of all bonding agents, laughter.

Both of us spoke of living together, and of an enduring relationship. It appeared we had established a comfort zone. I wanted to live with Marlene for a period of time before considering marriage again, and sought advice from a counselor friend, Kirsten. She told me that living together for one year was now the recommended practice. Marlene responded negatively and in writing. She wanted to go to the altar NOW!

I grew accustomed to her preference for expressing her unhappiness on paper rather than by direct confrontation. She wrote, "I do appreciate the fact that Kirsten is a 'counselor,' however I do not believe that she also has a degree as a marriage counselor." In no uncertain terms, Marlene pressed for marriage without living together. I talked to her about waiting until April for my decision.

Early in 1990, she wrote, "My darling, one day soon you will have the task of going into a store to buy a ring. I plan to be wearing your ring the rest of my life. Therefore I hope you'll consider what I like. Enclosed is a photo of the type of ring I hope to be wearing…As you know, by April you will have to voice your choice (coffee, tea or me?)…You're the best there is…"

Once again Marlene took exception to having to live together before marriage, and used an invitation to live with Dr. Weller as leverage.

"This is a secret," she said, "but Mrs. Weller is terminally ill. Mrs. Weller actually confided in me a few weeks ago. 'Marlene,' she said, 'I would rest easier knowing that you were here to take care of my husband after my death.' Brad, what should I do? Wallace Weller has been so good to me."

Marlene's stories always seemed to ring with such candor and sincerity. I accepted Marlene's "platonic relationship" with her male friends, and never asked her to disassociate from any of them.

Shortly thereafter, I phoned Lucille to tell her of my love for Marlene and that I was considering marriage. "I just dreamt that you had fallen in love with a European girl," she said, wishing me well.

One crisp, sunny morning that spring, a speeding car spooked Marlene's horse as she rode him along a roadside. The gelding reared and panicked, throwing her to the ground. Riderless, he galloped away, reins dragging in the sand. She suffered whiplash. Worse still, a portion of her left silicone breast implant was driven up under the collar bone.

Her repair surgery cost about $4,000, and she opted to have her implants enlarged. Short of cash, Marlene asked me for a loan of $2,500. She signed a promissory note, and I was impressed by her eventual diligence in repaying the loan.

*   *   *

I discovered that I might have a malignancy in March 1990. This came as an emotional and physical shock. There had been no history of cancer in my family, and I felt in my prime, full of life and vigor.

During the forthcoming days, Marlene was nowhere to be found. She was supposed to phone but never did. I left several messages and was mystified that there was no reply. This had raised questions of trust in my mind. Despite Marlene and I being lovers for three months, I contacted my ex-wife, Lucille, not Marlene, when my disease was firmly diagnosed as cancer. My positive-thinking philosophy helped me cope with setbacks in the past, but now I was apprehensive. It looked like the cancer could be terminal and I needed moral support.

In late April, I had surgery to remove superficial growths in my bladder. Fortunately, they were non-invasive, and hadn't been growing any longer than my tenure in Casa del Vista. As I had always been a non-smoker, it seemed possible that tap water from the bathroom might be the culprit. The bathroom side of the house was subsequently found to be toxic with carcinogens.

Lucille surprised me by arriving from the East Coast in her RV just prior to my surgery. At the hospital, flowers and cards came frequently from Marlene, who by then had learned of my cancer. These acts embarrassed me. Even more embarrassing were the calls from Marlene after my return home.

"I should be the one to take care of you," Marlene said. "I want nothing more than to be at your side."

Lucille had assumed the role of caretaker, visiting my home each day. She dutifully took me to doctors, cheered me through the difficult ordeal of chemotherapy, and golfed with me as often as I was up to it. Although Lucille remained in her RV, parked two miles away, she moved in again only following subsequent surgeries and chemotherapy.

Lucille knew that I was in an emotional quandary. We were both careful that there was no intimacy between us. To her credit, Lucille said that she was willing to step out of the picture if I opted for Marlene.

The month of May was to be decision-making time. At the end of the month, I wrote a note to Marlene:

"I need a TIME OUT with no final decision until a three month recovery period. I'm sorry to break off things with you now, because I need a CARETAKER in my life at this time. I need Lucille to add those elements of security and support required during the recovery period." Marlene counter-proposed that she also be given a three-month period, beginning September 1. I actually liked the idea, and informed Lucille. I suspected, of course, that Marlene would be looking for somebody else and probably already was. I was asked never to stop by her home during the summer unless she called me first.

Marlene kept calling me from her dental office. Throughout the summer she kept stressing, "I'm seeing only a few platonic old friends and am looking forward to being with you again September 1st."

I drove to Marlene's home on August 31, with the understanding that we would see one another beginning in September. It was 5:30 P.M. and she was just emerging from the garage.

"Oh," she said in a controlled tone, "This is a bad time. I'm expecting my ex-husband any minute now. He and his children are going to be staying with me for a couple of days. I'll call you after the weekend."

I asked why I hadn't heard from her, as I was no longer seeing Lucille. She replied, "I left a message for you this afternoon. I love you. Bye."

Were lies one of Marlene's trademarks? I was returning from out of town, so I hurried home to see what message had been left.

Sure enough, there was her cooing voice and her now-familiar reassurances. But Marlene, who had not visited my house for months, did not realize that my new answering machine announced the day and time of each call. She had left the message after I had seen her, and before I reached home.

It was time to move on.

The following week, I learned from Lucille that Marlene was living with a man named Luis. Marlene began driving a new car with a personalized license plate: LUIS2MAR. Luis to Marlene…what a gift!

I accepted Marlene's relationship and privately wished her well. But I had no hint how that relationship to Luis was to affect me in the future.

CHAPTER 3

▼

LUIS—THE ARTIST

Luis Rodriguez provided Marlene a long ride to a dead end. In correspondence to me, Marlene poured out her feelings about him:

"Luis is so good to me. He's 40 going on 15, a typical spoiled rich kid. All his life he got anything he wanted, and he recently sold his eight million dollar home in Bel Air. He is so-o-o-o much like a child…totally has a fascination with Disney characters, mystics and fantasy movies. After a while I may get tired of dealing with a child that is 40 years old…but I do love him more than I love life itself…and I feel so very lucky to have found this kind of real love. He makes me feel young, pretty and loved. While I had surgery, he took care of me like no man ever has in my life."

Luis was an artist. His vivid, large-format paintings had been shown in a Los Angeles gallery under the name of Paul Jacob Windom. But Luis didn't need to sell paintings to make a living, said Marlene. Not with the wealth of his parents.

Marlene confided:

"I met Luis at a party in Los Angeles this summer. He would commute all the way here just to have lunch with me. I saw him as a breath of fresh air…He's had 45 women, but he's the best lover ever. He has the sex drive of a 24-year-old…and oh, can he cook! He has dinner ready for me every night, then gives me a massage and plays his guitar…I feel lucky to have a man who truly loves me…I am going to marry him. Frankly, I have had it with the hunt-and-search game of life.

"I don't know why Luis wants to hold down a job washing windows in order to live with me. With all of his money, I don't know why he insists on working. He stands to inherit a bundle when his mom dies. He has a trust at age 45 to draw on with an amount I won't even mention, as it boggles my mind."

Luis passed himself off as the son of a wealthy British mother, but actually both of his parents were Mexican. His British accent, an annoyance to Mexicans, was acquired in England after getting a fine arts degree in California at Pasadena City College. He, like Marlene, had a flair for theatrics.

Marlene always maintained that her ideal man was "handsome, tall, trim, macho and sexy." But real love, as Marlene seemed to have found, does not usually fit the ideal image. Luis was ordinary looking, not handsome; chunky with a paunch, not trim; an indoor person, not athletic; but "very, very sexy."

By November, Marlene was less smitten. She said, "I'm not certain what Luis's real intentions are. I've decided to give it a little time…'til January…I don't know if I can resign myself to working for a living for five more years, and he says it will be five years before he receives the funds from his trust account in England that was left to him. His grandfather (Paul Windom Whitlock) owned the railroad there."

Later, Marlene phoned and asked if I could find a private investigator to check out some of the information Luis had provided. Although I had no intention of ever dating Marlene again, I was willing to help her solve a puzzling mystery. And doing this the right way was one of my fundamental tenets.

I found a P.I. who determined that Luis never had the eight million dollar residence in Bel Air, and was probably committing fraud in light of having two social security numbers, three driver's licenses, and two passports (U.S. and British). He told me that the case belonged with the U.S. Secret Service, not the FBI. The Secret Service confirmed this.

I knew Marlene was blindly in love with Luis and was having a hard time accepting his phoniness. Therefore, I took the matter directly to the Secret Service without her permission. The agency was sent a copy of Luis's birth certificate, Social Security earning records, DMV registration, a fairly recent photo, telephone records, and a three-page résumé that Marlene had drafted for Luis.

The information I supplied the Secret Service was referred to as "from THE SOURCE," in order that Marlene's name not be divulged. However, it wasn't long before they found out who she was, and about her live-in relationship with Luis.

Once the case was taken on by the Secret Service, I thought it would proceed to a rapid conclusion and that Luis would be brought to justice. Unknown to me was how skewed the U.S. Justice Department's operating system is.

The Mexican Master had filled his oil canvasses with clear and bright colors, but filled his record books with many aliases. Luis's account with the Bank of London proved to be non-existent, and he lied about graduating from Bradford University in England. Marlene even wanted to believe him when he said, "I'm mad at my mother because she bought me a hotel in England for Christmas. I wanted a Lear Jet."

Love can be blinding, but Marlene became more suspicious when Luis boasted, "My mother just sent me $10,000 as an allowance." Much later it was shown this money actually came from credit card fraud.

She said in late December that Luis was planning to move back to Los Angeles without her, but in February 1991, he had taken a new job with a prestigious desert art gallery. "I kept hoping my suspicions were wrong…when he got the job I figured he had gone straight."

My only encounter with Luis was in early May 1991. I was waiting in the reception area of a car service center in Palm Desert when a man entered and approached me.

"Are any of the attendants around?" he asked.

"I don't know where they went. Someone is probably out back," I replied.

At this point, I recognized Luis from his photo and from his British accent. He was wearing white Dockers pants with large pockets, and a crisp green-and-white striped dress shirt. He looked every inch the model of a modern gentleman.

I watched closely as Luis returned to the front desk and an attendant entered from the back. "Curtis," greeted the attendant, "your car is ready." Luis spoke in his clipped British accent about a warranty covering part of the repair costs. I watched him leave in a new gray Nissan 300Z.

The clerk confirmed that his customer had used the name Curtis Turner, and had earlier presented a credit card to that effect. Without doubt this had to be Luis, the consummate deceiver.

"Oh dear," said Marlene softly, as I recounted the story. "He had a big wad of twenty-dollar bills, and told me he was going to pay in cash for the car repair."

Curtis Turner was a very familiar name in the desert. A 65-year-old multimillionaire, he was an elegant and unfailingly courteous silver-haired gentleman, rumored to have made a vast fortune in Nevada real estate. He and his wife, Fanny, owned several residences, and had made a strong impression in Palm Springs society when they began construction of a $25 million dollar desert estate.

Curtis Turner's car collection was legendary. Housed in a subterranean garage, it contained many priceless antiques, including a variety of vintage Rolls Royces. All were reportedly registered in Nevada, where Fanny owned a casino.

Curtis and Fanny Turner were also patients of Dr. Randolph. Marlene was in charge of patient files, and was custodian of confidential data on every patient.

"Marlene," I asked, "do you think Luis is using you to gain access to Dr. Randolph's records?"

"He asked me who were the richest clients in the office," she responded quickly.

"Have you supplied Luis with information about Curtis Turner?" I asked.

"No," she said. "But I remember one Saturday when I was running errands, I left my office keys on the table. I didn't discover until later that day that he had taken them. He admitted taking them, but said it had been by mistake. He must have used them to enter Dr. Randolph's office."

"Isn't there a security system at the office?" I asked.

"No, and he must have known that," Marlene replied.

Her response mystified me, but I gave Marlene the benefit of the doubt. After all, Marlene had submitted all of the evidence against Luis, and had given lip service to apprehending and jailing him for his wrong-doing. I did not like that she was still so closely involved with a con artist, even if she could count herself as one of his victims. But didn't Marlene know better?

Marlene also suspected that Luis was cheating on her. She wrote me a note about her feelings:

"I must be nuts to want a guy who is so cruel, selfish, uncaring, and a phony in all ways. How do I get myself back on track? Maybe I need a shrink. Heck, I cry over him…how did I get so dependent?"

She promised to keep a more vigilant eye on Luis, and to confront him when she felt comfortable doing so.

"Luis asked if the Curtis Turners had moved into their new house," she told me later in May. Luis then added that he was aware the Turners were about to receive three million dollars from the First Bank of Las Vegas.

"The Turners' account in the local bank had dropped from $162,000 to a $72,000 deficit," Luis had said to Marlene, "and the credit card ring is letting me take all the blame."

Marlene said that she had looked in Luis's briefcase and found blank checks belonging to the Turners. "They were 'Superfund' checks issued by a local bank," she said.

I was, of course, in contact with the Secret Service about this. Their response was disappointing. The agents professed that this was just one of many cases like it, and that their priorities lay in protective work for the White House. If the total amount of fraud could be proven in excess of $100,000, then stiffer penalties might be assessed. But it seemed to me they were doing very little.

Moreover, I didn't particularly like the fact that if this case were to go to court, I would be a chief witness. Did that put me in danger? Marlene also worried that I could become a victim of Luis's anger and retaliation, or that he might try to reach my own investment accounts.

I was slightly reassured by the Secret Service, who said that perpetrators of fraud usually do not commit murder. Besides, if revenge were exacted by Luis or the credit card ring, wouldn't it be against THE SOURCE, Marlene?

"Luis claims the immigration authorities are after him under the guise of Paul Windom," reported Marlene. "He resents my asking so many questions."

Luis moved back to Los Angeles in mid-1991. Marlene gave Luis an ultimatum of one week to indicate whether he wanted to reconcile and give up his old life.

"If not, he can drop dead! I'm not waiting around. He still professes love for me, but he said we're incompatible and that I'm too inquisitive."

Luis phoned her from Los Angeles the following week.

"What are you doing in Los Angeles?" she asked.

"I'm getting the third degree from you again," said Luis.

"That was an innocent question," said Marlene.

"See, we can't even get along in a phone conversation!" Luis shot back.

Marlene claimed that she never heard from him again, although he had promised another conversation in August. She thought he had taken up with another girl, or that he had gone to England to lay low.

Marlene was devastated. She composed a long letter to Luis to vent her feelings: "Do you actually have a heart, a soul? You got what you came for, lots of money. You didn't even call me on August 12th like you promised. It's all over…" The letter was never sent.

That month, Marlene became worried when Curtis Turner's wife came to the dentist's office and, without speaking to her, had a private conference with Dr. Randolph.

This was just the beginning of complaints against Marlene by dental patients. For weeks, the good doctor, a very quiet and studious person, said nothing to Marlene as she fretted about her fate. Finally, she approached him after work and asked whether she was going to be fired.

"The situation is under review," Dr. Randolph told her.

The termination was official in December. Marlene blamed the Turners for starting rumors about her.

"I loved my job and hated to leave," she told me. The stress of the situation had hampered her job performance. Her previous high-quality accounting skills had deteriorated.

Marlene filed a small claims lawsuit against Luis Rodriguez on December 31, 1991, asking for damages in the amount of $5,000. In court papers, she stated that she was fired from her job of three and a half years after Luis appropriated information from the files at the dental office where she worked, and used the information to defraud patients.

In the Plaintiff's Statement to the Clerk of the Small Claims Court, Marlene wrote: "Defendant is wanted by the Secret Service for FRAUD and grand theft."

Luis vanished, and the process servers couldn't find him. Because Marlene did not pursue the case, it was dismissed.

Luis managed to get the most bang out of his buck. The problem was he had larceny in his heart, and the bucks were wrested away from others. He was not only an artist of conventional oil paintings, but an unconventional con artist supreme.

CHAPTER 4

NEW COUPLINGS AND BURIED LIES

Maybe it was her sweet smile and her gentle way.
Maybe it was romantic sharing and understanding.
Maybe it was her charm and affectionate mannerisms.
Maybe it was her aura of a sophisticated lady.

Marlene fit the mold. She had no difficulty finding new lovers, including Bernardo Gouthier, the well-known playboy bachelor from Rio de Janeiro. While Marlene and I were first dating between November 1989 and April 1990, she considered his 20-acre Coral Tree Ranch to be one of her private retreats.

A handsome six-footer with dark hair and piercing eyes, he was viewed as a Brazilian John F. Kennedy, Jr., the scion of a wealthy and famous family. In his early 40s, Bernardo had a large inheritance that enabled him to own a modeling agency in Paris, and to transform his horse ranch into an impressive showplace for art and sculpture.

Bernardo was known and respected as an "artist eccentric." He would invite enamored young girls to see the paintings displayed in his home. At one major art gallery show in Palm Desert that winter, he was the only local artist represented.

Marlene would spend hours riding with Bernardo, describing him as a wonderful instructor. I discovered later his major instruction courses were Sex 101, Sex 201 and Sex 301.

When asked if there had been an "urge to merge" with Bernardo, she replied, "Oh no, he's just a business client. He really prefers much younger girls in their 20s. You know, this morning when I was out there to ride alone, he had one of his girls there. I paid Bernardo $1,200 for my horse, Billy, and also pay him a $200 boarding fee each month. Billy's an Appaloosa quarter horse. He's great in strength and stamina. It's incredible. A ride of four hours doesn't tire him out at all."

Marlene would always divert conversations from Bernardo to horses. The question had not entered my mind whether the horse trading might be a case of bartering for services. Nor did I know that by the end of April, she had returned the horse to Bernardo, and another girlfriend was now riding on Billy. Although Marlene was with new friends on their horses at the polo grounds, she would visit Bernardo periodically.

Bernardo would not remain in Marlene's life long. He was murdered in 1997 at his ranch. His financial struggles to keep open a Sculpture Park had been publicized widely, and rumors about his drug dealing had intensified. The Sheriff's office had a number of suspects.

*   *   *

In May of 1990, an old boyhood chum, Tex Gilman, visited me at Casa del Vista. We golfed together for a couple of days, and I confided my dilemma of deciding between Lucille and Marlene. It was a heart-to-heart discussion, which ended with my accepting his suggestion that I look further afield.

A small voice in the back of my head kept saying, "Stay away from Marlene no matter how attracted you are to her." Why was she such a secretive person?

Lucille helped keep Marlene in proper perspective: "Marlene is just a sexual butterfly. She wouldn't make a good wife." I realized Marlene was a free spirit, but certainly not promiscuous.

Time and time again, I would be reminded of the adage, "You treat someone like what they mean to you." The trouble was my heart spoke louder than my mind. Whenever I talked to Marlene by phone, that particular day would become Valentine's Day. This explorer definitely needed a new compass heading.

That September, the week after Luis settled in with Marlene, I invited Lucille to take an Arizona trip with me. I was delighted when she offered to drive her spacious RV. Lucille arrived in the desert earlier than expected on that Friday afternoon. In my absence, she wondered if I was replanning a September reunion with Marlene. Worried that I might be over at Marlene's, she located her address and drove there.

Lucille knocked and introduced herself to Marlene.

"Do you still love Brad?" she asked directly.

"No, I did, but I don't now," Marlene answered. "I have a boyfriend living here with me. See the red Jeepster out front? That belongs to him and he's living here now. Frankly," she added, "you can have Brad yourself. Take him!"

"I'm not shopping," Lucille replied. "But I don't know what's going on. Brad is ill—ill with cancer, and I just don't want him harmed. I want what's best for him."

Lucille extended her hand and Marlene took it warmly.

"It's too bad we had to meet under these circumstances," Marlene said. "I'll be glad to talk to you some more any time you'd like. Give me a call at Dr. Randolph's office, and we'll have lunch together."

The two women, both blonde and similar in age, confirmed that these words were spoken, as recorded by Lucille's hand. The pair had a habit of keeping records, and making private records of conversations. Fortunately, I did, too.

When I returned late that afternoon, I found Lucille's RV parked in front. Lucille was inside Casa del Vista, mad as a hornet. My extensive private files were strewn about, including notes on Marlene and Lucille. It was apparent that Lucille had seen my ledger sheet, "Pros and Cons for Lucille and Marlene." Finally, I calmed her down, and surprisingly, we departed that evening for Arizona where we spent a wonderful weekend with Tex and Mary Gilman. A crisis had turned into an enjoyable trip. I made no promises nor proposals, but it was understood, for now, Lucille had returned to "Number One" status.

When Lucille purchased a small desert home in November, I was puzzled. She disliked the desert, and had professed that her home was wherever she parked her RV. She confided later that the reason was her desire to live close to me.

*   *   *

I was still trying to follow the advice of Tex, and had submitted a new ad to the *Los Angeles Times*. Later, I spied another ad in the <u>Times</u> that appealed to me. It began with the headline *GOLF*. It was from a woman who shared my interests, and had blue-ribbon credits.

Maggie, the golfer, narrowed down her response list from 100 to six, then phoned me. This was the beginning of a romance that included theater trips to Los Angeles, and a visit to San Francisco for the World Series that fall. Periodically, Maggie and I would see each other at our respective residences. Maggie had homes both in the desert and in a San Diego suburb.

Unfortunately, watchdog Lucille learned of my dating Maggie and was duly concerned. Maggie, after all, was a raven-haired beauty. More important, Maggie was charming, affectionate and a good companion.

However, Maggie and I had made no commitment to one another, and were admittedly dating others.

In late January 1991, Marlene phoned and wanted to know what the prospects were for connecting again. This question came out of the blue. Cautiously, I proceeded to compose a list of questions for her to answer about trust issues.

Lucille somehow found out about this and admonished me, "When you get a lemon, make lemonade." She wanted to be the lemonade *and* sweetener for me.

Soon thereafter, Marlene dropped by to see me on her way home from a visit to her friendly landlord. She said she would like to resume our relationship, and wondered whether she could move in after Luis left town. I replied negatively, and told her there was no chance. When Luis left her a month later, she broke her lease.

She phoned me after she moved and asked if I knew any available men. I suggested she place a personal ad in the newspaper. She decided not only to place a local ad, but to join a singles video dating service.

In April I called Maggie to tell her I now felt committed to Lucille most of all, and would not be able to accept her invitation to be her host at a large party she was giving. Privately, I had discussed with my family my difficulty in deciding between the three women, Lucille, Maggie and Marlene.

"Lucille made a wonderful caretaker," I told them, "but I don't have the same feelings for her or Maggie that I have for Marlene." However, Marlene's association with a con artist made me nervous.

Through the video service, Marlene established another relationship during the summer of 1991. Nick Celani was a 58-year-old Italian lothario.

"I couldn't believe how many women this Casanova had married until he showed me the private files he kept in a built-in safe," Marlene said. "Nick has over 20 divorces!" We both laughed.

"He plans to marry an Oriental woman who's having trouble emigrating to the United States," Marlene said. "My relationship with Nick remains platonic, and I'm really not interested in him. He's pot-bellied and not my type."

By November, Marlene was driving a brand new sports car. She believed that you are what you drive. Her new car had to be a sleek one, a sports car that maneuvered like she did through life: a car like an XJ6 with a sun roof and all the extras. With the exhilaration of the desert air and personalized license plate, MARSXJ6, she'd impulsively cut in front of the car ahead if it caught her fancy. *Fwoom!* She loved to accelerate, pop in a romantic cassette, and feel forever young. Her most fervent wish was to stop the world so she would never grow older.

She made it appear in conversation that the new car belonged to her. Owning such a fancy and eye-catching number meant a great deal. But her alleged ownership raised eyebrows at the dental office, particularly when it was discovered that Luis had been swindling some of the patients.

*   *   *

Marlene and I each looked in different directions, but Lucille couldn't. It was still difficult for her to consider being anyone other than Mrs. Brad Dunaway. My children, however, were warning me about resuming an intimate relationship with Lucille because they didn't trust her. I preferred to think that Brad Dunaway knew what he was doing. He didn't.

I became preoccupied with a book I was writing slated for summer publication. Lucille accompanied me on a number of trips, including one to the American Booksellers Convention in New York City, where I signed copies of my book. Lucille was so sparkling and cooperative that it appeared she was now fulfilling the promises she had carefully drafted in writing. I reasoned that if we could get along as well as this for a month or two, I might consider her proposed remarriage.

Lucille found out in June that I was still having occasional lunches with Marlene in the desert. These lunches were related to the ongoing Secret Service investigation of Luis, but Lucille was bothered by the association and could not forget or forgive. We both wondered if we should remarry.

Lucille assured me that if a remarriage didn't work, our previous financial settlement would prevail. Furthermore, she suggested that if we decided to divorce again, it would be amicable and without attorneys. We later signed an agreement that we both believed was fair. Either one could step out of the marriage within five years without further financial penalty or dissent.

However, even on the last day before we flew to Hawaii in July, I hadn't made up my mind about remarrying. I had wanted to join my brother and family in Hawaii, and was still considering options when our entourage arrived in the Islands. And I was still on cloud nine with the initial success of my book. In past years I thought of myself as bold; in Maui I felt empowered to take on the world.

It was the ninth inning, the bases were loaded, and two were out when I came up to bat on July 7, 1991. I went for the home run and struck out. We were remarried!

When I make a mistake, it's a *beaut*!

I thought Lucille had changed, but a week after the wedding, it was apparent that her old character had returned. She scolded, she tried to manage my life in great detail, and she was critical of my every decision. Admittedly, I was following my own agenda. Any mention by me of having had a lunch out would make Lucille furious.

The clouds on the horizon became thunderheads. It seemed Lucille made a Supreme Court case out of the smallest of issues. Intimacy suffered. After a month of marriage, it was lost completely.

When Lucille brought her ailing mother out to the desert from the Midwest, the strain became unbearable. I suggested the visit be no longer than two to three weeks, but Lucille insisted on four months. Because I was fond of my mother-in-law, and aware that she had never been told about our divorce and subsequent remarriage, I didn't want to hurt her while she was my guest. Consequently, I decided to postpone notifying Lucille that I was again seeking a divorce until after her mother returned home.

After Christmas, Lucille and her mother departed together in the RV for a trip to Florida. I was unable to talk divorce until early in 1992. When I flew to Florida, I discovered my mother-in-law had accepted a ride back to the Midwest. Lucille was now in her RV, unprepared for my bad news. She was clearly crushed. She had clung to the flimsy thread that existed between us. I thought there would be no recriminations, no bad memories and no attorneys. How wrong could I be?

When Lucille was formally served on April 1, it was not intended that the petition for divorce arrive on April Fools Day. She reluctantly accepted the papers and moved all of her belongings back to her desert residence. It was again peaceful—for a time.

CHAPTER 5

▼

PITFALL FOR BRAD

"Is Marlene Washington an accessory in the Luis Rodriguez case?"

In April 1992, I met with an agent from the Secret Service. Was Marlene part of the credit card ring? Was she under suspicion?

"I don't think so," the Secret Service agent replied, looking me straight in the eye.

With Lucille out of the picture, I needed some advice. Marlene was still a part of my romantic imagination. But I did not want to be courting trouble, and was very nervous about Marlene's association with Luis.

I was relieved to hear an unequivocal "all clear" from the Secret Service. If the agent had hinted otherwise, I was planning to hire a private investigator to investigate Marlene on my own. Unfortunately, my previous experience with a P.I., whom I had hired in 1989 on Marlene's behalf, had left a bad taste in my mouth. The detective had not responded to some requests, and much of his work was not timely or completed.

Through 1992, I continued to make efforts to bring Luis Rodriguez to justice. There was substantial evidence of fraud, theft, and credit card forgery. Even so, I began to hear glib excuses about the slow progress of the case. "This type of thing happens all the time," I was told.

The previous year, a letter from my Congressman had spurred renewed attention from the Secret Service, but the matter was again put on the back burner. The agent who initiated the investigation was replaced in mid-1992, and the new agent said he didn't know when an indictment would be filed. Would the case die on the vine, while this criminal continued to commit fraud in the Los Angeles area and perhaps nationwide?

*   *   *

After being terminated by Dr. Randolph, Marlene sought new employment in early 1992. Normally, she would have been able to step into another dental position, but now her prospects were not encouraging. She grew depressed, but in April finally secured a position at the Polo Club as receptionist and secretary.

Marlene was also somewhat unhappy about the results of her breast repair surgery the previous September. Although I could see only an unobtrusive blemish and certainly no significant scar, Marlene said, "I need recompense." She filed a malpractice suit against her well-regarded plastic surgeon, seeking $35,000 to $40,000 in damages.

Marlene and I had conferred endlessly about Luis and his credit card scheme. But I still didn't understand why Marlene had been terminated by Dr. Randolph. Concerned, I met the dentist for the first time in his luxurious Palm Desert office.

"Is there any evidence," I asked him, "that Marlene was actually an accomplice to Luis Rodriguez?"

Dr. Randolph was soft spoken and reticent. Tall and good-looking, I could see why he attracted a loyal following among the desert's elite. He could not have been more diplomatic.

"I had to defer to my clients's wishes," Dr. Randolph said. "It was a difficult decision for me to make."

Dr. Randolph was hesitant to say any more.

Dissatisfied with the doctor's response, I called Fanny and Curtis Turner, the clients who had come to the dentist with their suspicions about Marlene. Although Fanny Turner once answered the phone and promised to let her husband know I wanted to be in touch, I never heard from Curtis Turner. Several subsequent messages went unreturned.

I never found any evidence that Marlene shared Luis's guilt. And yet, in my lucid moments, I believed that a renewed romance with Marlene was simply out of the question. I didn't like that she had been associated with a con man, and was reluctant to date her.

My mind turned to another con artist victim, my friend Nanette. This 35-year-old was the granddaughter of a famous golfer, whose biography I authored. As a Hawaiian teenager, she had been selected "Miss Personality" in a nationwide contest. Nanette became a superb schoolteacher, honored and respected by her peers.

Returning to her native Hawaii in 1988 after a traumatic California divorce, Nanette rapidly fell in love with a 6'7" "Tarzan hulk."

"I'm mesmerized by this Tom Selleck look-alike," she told me before I took the couple to a beachside restaurant in Maui. "I hope you like Raymond."

Although a bit self-laudatory, Raymond was a personable 40-ish Adonis. The two made a handsome pair, I thought.

Despite family opposition, Nanette married Raymond that summer in Hawaii. He brought her to San Francisco where they lived for a short time. She was still unaware of Raymond's scams, one of which was the illegal acquisition of an Oklahoma ranch where they moved in 1990. Raymond had already exhausted Nanette's prior savings of $150,000 and was now rapidly depleting her credit card limits.

Unexpectedly, he decided to return to California. Nanette did not understand why Raymond drove such a hurried and circuitous route, pausing in Sheridan, Wyoming. It was there that the law caught up with Raymond. He was jailed after his arrest for fraud and multiple scams.

Nanette was shocked by this turn of events. However, she was still the loyal and loving wife. After hocking all her valuables, she was barely able to raise Raymond's bond of $1,400.

A few days after his release, he admitted that he didn't love her. Raymond threatened harm, then tried to abandon her. It was the dead of winter in the cold north of Sheridan.

Nanette was desperate. While Raymond was in the shower, she took his only pair of shoes, his boots, and escaped to the police station. Raymond was quickly apprehended and rearrested.

Finally, he was returned in custody to Oklahoma for trial. This time Nanette and the scam victims pressed charges. Raymond was convicted and sentenced to two 4-year terms, a sentence that was later shortened to 16 months.

When I met with Nanette in Ardmore, Oklahoma in early 1991, she dreaded the day Raymond would be free.

"Oh, the nightmare I lived! I never realized what a sociopath he is. Now I fear for my life."

It seemed obvious that Raymond was a professional gigolo, hustler and criminal, just like Luis. If an exceptional person like Nanette could be fooled, Marlene might also have been innocently trapped and blind-sided. I began to sympathize with the troubled world of con artists' victims.

Later that year, Nanette, by then remarried and enjoying her honeymoon, stayed at Casa del Vista. She grew to know Marlene well and liked her. The two women not only exchanged stories about their respective con artists, but remained in touch by mail.

*   *   *

By April 1992, Marlene had written me a long letter detailing her feelings.

"I still live in fear wondering what Luis may pull next...I have but one wish: that the day I have to testify in court, I can stand up and give my name as Marlene Dunaway. That would make me feel so proud and so secure, knowing I belong to YOU. You are the kindest, most caring person I have ever known, and had it not been for the cancer thing, you and I would be as one today. You know I'll be happy to go on working, I don't want to be a burden to you financially...You and I share so much in how we feel and what we love to do...I want you in all ways."

Marlene and I began to date seriously, but not before HIV tests relieved my chief concern about her liaisons with Luis. During this dating period she asked:

"Brad, do you know the reason I took up with Luis?"

"Why," I asked.

"It was to get even with you," she said. "For tossing me to the wind when you took Lucille back."

I was beginning to see a pattern in Marlene, a pattern of self-punishment. It made sense to think Marlene had thrown herself into an abusive relationship on the heels of our own broken romance.

Marlene could see that I was still attracted to her, and never made any secret of her own affection. This time, however, Marlene knew better than to force her hand. She knew I would not initiate any physical contact before I was entirely comfortable with her.

Most important, Marlene recognized my hesitancy to marry again. This time, she accepted my reservations, and was forthright about not putting any pressure on me to commit:

"I want you to know how much I appreciate how you stood by me while I was going through the worst time with the Luis Rodriquez dilemma. You were my hero, and there to listen. It was this that made me fall in love with you all over again. You gave me the hope to go on...I'm so glad the divorce from Lucille is just around the corner. I am counting the days tell we can be

together, each day and each night. And I'll promise you—I'll never pressure you into marriage."

Marlene's forthrightness brought her that much closer. I was relieved she was willing to discuss subjects, particularly trust issues, which had previously been off limits.

Within short order, Marlene surprised me with a *Cohabitation Agreement* she had drafted for my inspection. The agreement said, "I will devote considerable time, skill, service, industry and effort during cohabitation to the investment and management of properties and income…"

She wrote that both parties would "promise to be true-blue, and honest about all contacts with past friends (of either sex), and that no secret meetings with ex-spouses or pals shall take place," a promise I naively believed.

"True-blue," said the agreement. It was vintage Marlene.

Written agreements with Lucille had worked well so far, so I felt reassured. Marlene's offer was very tempting. Her proposal protected me from any financial complication, particularly with my financial consultant looking over her shoulder. In addition, Marlene was willing "to share household expenses and duties of home care."

Most important, how could I lose if the agreement included a 30-day notification clause for separation?

We sat down together and developed our *Living Together Contract*. In its opening paragraph, the agreement stated: "Each of us enters into this agreement without having sought legal counsel other than the book, *The Living Together Kit*." The book was compiled by lawyers who specialized in such work. Marlene's "true-blue" language, relating to past friends and secret meetings with ex-spouses, was incorporated directly into the contract, as was the 30-day notice, in a separate section.

"Brad and Marlene commit themselves to one another as lovers, friends and housemates, with the promise that kindness, goodwill, and sense of humor shall guide them through both the rainbows and rainstorms in the days ahead."

Marlene moved into Casa del Vista on June 1, 1992, three days after we signed the agreement. From the start, our home radiated happiness.

Most of all, I felt Marlene's complete devotion. "I love you more each day," she inscribed on photos, sent to me by mail even after we were living together.

This was the woman who loved me, and whom I loved, as much as life itself.

CHAPTER 6

NEW MARRIAGE?

"Rise! Soar!"

Although we went to church only on special occasions, I remember clearly the Easter service and its message. Marlene enthusiastically took part and sang in full voice. Praise welled up from deep inside her, resonating joyfully.

"Rise, Rise, Rise and Soar!!!"

The religious part of Marlene would evaporate as soon as we hit the parking lot. But for a moment, Marlene felt a passionate intensity. This intensity was one of her most beguiling qualities.

She had won her place in my home and heart. Before, she had been a salmon swimming upstream against the current. Now she was headed downstream on an exciting whitewater adventure. I was along for the ride, and quite frankly, enjoying every minute of it.

The whole atmosphere changed when Marlene moved into Casa del Vista. The two of us lived a charmed existence. I was absorbed in all things

Marlene: she was funny and spontaneous, but never less than affectionate or considerate towards me.

Whereas Lucille and I occasionally raised our voices in anger, the decibel levels with Marlene never rose, and we maintained a calm composure. We were both good listeners, and didn't tend to correct or control. Although physically attracted to Marlene from the beginning, I grew to love her for the values I considered most important: close friendship, shared interests, and an emphasis on integrity, chivalry and family.

We were typical desertoids, living in our sparkling Coachella Valley, surrounded by our colorful and ever-fascinating mountain terrain. Desertoids wear shorts all year and do their shopping at Wal-Mart or K-Mart. They know the savory and affordable restaurants, and usually prefer these to the array of caviar cuisines. Desertoids have a ready supply of anecdotes about Bob Hope, and point out his unique hillside home to visiting relatives. They attend the Golf Cart Parade in Palm Desert, the only city that allows golf carts on its streets.

Desertoids write letters to the editor galore, and are passionately interested in the preservation of bighorn sheep in the adjacent mountains. Desertoids feed the hummingbirds and roadrunners, and do their grocery shopping after dark under the canopy of shimmering stars.

With Marlene, all of my priorities were re-arranged. I was so devoted to making her happy that I would often drop my own plans at a moment's notice and accompany her. Like co-conspirators in the intrigue of love, we shared private faces in public places, and at home, relished every moment of intimacy. Marlene was invariably tender and giving. My commitment to her increased by the day. I was mesmerized.

On a typical summer morning, we would ride our bikes at dawn as the mountains gleamed in their orange alpine glow, and the desert sun sent streamers of crimson across the morning sky. Marlene and I would then swim together, or play water volleyball, enjoying the intoxicating fragrance of the jasmine, honeysuckle and gardenias. I was amused that Marlene made me play from the deep end of the pool. As I squinted into the sun, she could playfully go for the spike. In the evenings, we enjoyed private dancing lessons together. Everything we did was part of a beautiful dance, a romance that continued to deepen.

The love sparks flew. At home, I initiated the most hugs, Marlene the most sex. It seemed the more stimulation we received from the other, the more our intimacy increased. Our days were magic, our nights filled with enchanted moonlight. How could it get any better?

I spoke to Marlene about our having 20 more years of wonderful love-making. Remembering her mother's early death from breast cancer, Marlene invariably reduced the number of years to ten. As optimistic as Marlene was most of the time, she felt a deep-seated fatalism about her own health and longevity. Was this all the more reason, perhaps, to live each moment to its fullest?

That summer I made an interesting observation. It is human nature not to admit an oversight or mistake, but Marlene carried this to an extreme. She never said, "I goofed," "I messed up," or "How absent-minded of me." She simply couldn't bring herself to admit, or even hint, that any action was her fault.

A good example of this quirk came after she lost a box of private journals and pictures. She had spent a month or two looking for the box, and had even asked if I was the culprit. One night, when I phoned from out-of-town, she joyously reported its discovery.

"I found my big box of pictures!" she said.

"Where was it?" I asked.

"The gremlins got it!" said Marlene.

Gremlins: they were her common answer, and excuse, for anything that went wrong. For both of us, the gremlins soon became the scapegoat for mislaid objects and minor misdeeds alike.

Marlene left her job at the Polo Club in June. She had held the position of receptionist and secretary for only a few months, complaining that her boss was a "nit-picker" and that she had "worked her buns off" for her. I knew her true talents were in bookkeeping and dentistry, so I supported her decision to leave a dead-end position.

Marlene offered to do my own computer work. However, I felt it best to take most of my work to a secretarial service. This protected me from becoming a "nit-picker" as well.

Summertime meant travel time. We took many journeys together, long and short, and it was comforting to have Marlene along even for business trips. Her soft purr and easy laughter were always a source of satisfaction.

Marlene favored pricey restaurants and top hotels. She accepted my habit of taking lower-priced airlines, and leaving from distant airports rather than the local and expensive Palm Springs air terminal. But her champagne tastes were obvious. She favored idyllic hideaway spots in Hawaii, Fiji and Tahiti, and shelved my idea of a wilderness trek to arctic Alaska. At each destination, Marlene anticipated a gift from me after window-shopping all the boutiques.

Marlene behaved as if she were beginning a dream marriage. She took a deep interest in redoing my home. She designed new furniture for our master bedroom, and redecorated other rooms. A long list of proposed improvements was submitted to me. Her vocabulary did not include the terms "household budget" and "cost overruns," but I usually let Marlene have her way.

Photographs of Marlene dominated the master bedroom. The walls of the large walk-in closet were covered with them. She even hung a framed composite of herself at the entrance to the bedroom suite.

A visiting handyman once gasped at the display.

"So many pictures of her—and they all look so different!"

It was true. Marlene looked different in every one of them. Many of Marlene's photographs were taken when she was a model in her earlier years. She continued to possess an amazing chameleon-like quality, an ability to change her appearance at will. Just as she erased all traces of her German accent when she came to Canada at sixteen, she could reinvent her looks to suit the time and place. It was a magical gift.

I had virtually overcome my prior reservations about Marlene. I was madly in love, and believed life could not get any better. Still faithful to the *Living Together Contract*, I had made an additional promise to my children that I would wait a year before marrying again. My divorce from Lucille was to become final in September.

Yet on out of town trips, Marlene would introduce herself as "Brad's fiancée," and it became quite natural to think of her that way. I never corrected her. There was little doubt that the altar was just a step away.

I thanked the fates that steered me
To my Casa with mountain views,
To spend what time is left for me
In an Eden of rosy hues.

CHAPTER 7

▼

POSTPONED DREAMS

In September, the day after our divorce was to be finalized, I received a card from Lucille: "Congratulations on *your* divorce! Justice *will* prevail in the end."

What was that supposed to mean?

Later, I discovered that the courts had misled us to think the divorce became final that month. Another legal form still had to be signed by both parties.

"Oh no!" I thought, realizing this could initiate delaying tactics.

During the summer, Lucille had left many irate phone messages. She had become desperate as the economy worsened, and was troubled that I was so hard to reach by phone.

"You have ruined my life," she complained. I knew that if Lucille discovered Marlene was living with me, her anger would know no bounds.

How much could I depend upon Lucille's professed integrity and on our prior written agreements? In late October, I found out. Lucille went to an attorney, who tried to break the earlier divorce agreement and obtain spousal support to bolster the large settlement already paid.

Lucille's attorney told me our signed agreements meant little. She was free to use an attorney in the second divorce action, despite her written agreement to the contrary, because everyone has the right of legal counsel. Although her lawyer conceded that Lucille had agreed to no additional settlement unless our marriage lasted five years, he insisted that Lucille was now unemployable and needed alimony. He suggested I seek my own legal counsel.

A major snag was that the hearing date had been set by Lucille's attorney for later that month. I phoned him and obtained assurance that the hearing would be postponed until December, as I had a November deadline for finishing my latest book. No written confirmation of the extension was immediately received. When it did arrive, a proviso had been added that I pay Lucille $5,000 *up front*. Quickly, I jumped into action and secured the services of the most reputable family law attorney in the desert.

Marlene was especially upset. Although she didn't articulate it, I could sense she wondered how much of a financial drain Lucille might impose. Perhaps Marlene feared her dreams of matrimony were fading. A sizeable death benefit package had been provided for Lucille when I married her, and Marlene undoubtedly expected the same treatment. It certainly looked as if the final divorce from Lucille wouldn't materialize soon.

Marlene remained outwardly upbeat. She said she looked forward to traveling extensively with me, even though the court proceedings might drag out to December or January.

A turning point for Marlene occurred in late September, when she herself appeared in court for a hearing related to her termination by Dr. Randolph. I could tell Marlene was disappointed with a judgment that curtailed her disability payments. She didn't elaborate on what had happened in court. "I'm over it," she said. "It's cold coffee."

A day later, we departed for a week at Lake Tahoe, where we took some side trips and had an exhilarating time horseback riding and walking on the beach. I introduced Marlene to friends at a professional meeting as my fiancée.

After our return, I received a letter from her:

"My dearest Brad…it is with great sadness that I write this letter to you, and I feel deeply depressed, wondering what there is in life that keeps dealing me so much pain and hardships along the way—the sad fact is that I can go on no longer keeping our financial agreement. I need to look for a job and hope that the money comes soon from the settlements that I am due."

Marlene was referring to three settlements: one from her "botched" breast repair surgery, a second from a friend's estate, and the third from her disability benefits. The first two were yet to be resolved, and the third had obviously fallen far short of her expectations.

Marlene offered a number of options for loaning her money. I chose instead to give her a credit card for her future purchases. She thanked me for my support, and renewed her pledge of love.

Thus far, we had both met our financial obligations. Marlene took charge of paying all the household bills from my account, reporting the check numbers and amounts to my financial manager. I had shown her all of my financial records in accordance with the *Living Together Contract*, but so far Marlene had remained tight-lipped about her own financial affairs. She kept them a secret.

Marlene created a mirage of means. I interpreted her sports car, her horse, and her patronage of high-fashion stores as evidence of a sizeable bank account. She pored over *Vogue, Mirabella, Elle, Elegance* and *Allure* magazines, and in all had fifteen magazine subscriptions. I could tell she was consumed with fashion: the clothes, the models, the poses. Marlene also said she wanted to buy a piano for our home to replace the one Lucille had taken, and that she planned to contribute paintings and sculptures.

It had not even occurred to me that this could be a misleading show-off pattern, or worse yet, a grubstake for mining more gold claims. After all, following her emergency surgery two years before, Marlene had conscientiously repaid my loan of $2,500.

Marlene loved to show me magazine advertisements for attractive country ranch estates, with stables and riding grounds. She suggested I sell Casa del Vista and buy one of these country ranches. Although a small horse ranch would cost a fraction of my home's worth, I could not bear the thought of leaving the place my family and I so dearly loved. I listened patiently, but could not justify moving. Why did Marlene keep returning to the subject?

*　　　　　*　　　　　*

Everett, Marlene's son, was an irregular visitor to Casa del Vista and often brought his girlfriend. In his early 20s, Everett had long unkempt hair and a sullen demeanor. He kept mysterious hours, and often appeared unexpectedly. A high school dropout who had lived in Northern California for several years, Everett had once hoped to become a Navy Seal. Although he no longer had a precise career plan, he was fruitlessly trying to earn a high school diploma.

One of Everett's favorite phrases was "I don't do mornings." He didn't do afternoons or evenings, either. Although little impressed with Everett's conversational ability, I remember one bizarre dinner during which he talked non-stop, performing what amounted to a stand-up comedy routine.

Everett's girlfriend had such a harsh look that she appeared considerably older than her 17 years. She was short and chunky, with straggly brown hair framing a haggard, swollen face.

After some months, Marlene asked if I would terminate my gardener and hire Everett. Although it was difficult to refuse Marlene's request, I did. My current gardener's performance was acceptable, and in truth, I was not always comfortable with Everett. At best, Everett was unpredictable.

*　　　　　*　　　　　*

A melancholy began to creep into Marlene's personality. Her interest in talking about Lucille and Luis waned. In fact, she no longer wanted to hear their names mentioned. Although she had never missed a chance to travel, she began declining to go on some out-of-town trips. Several vacations had to be canceled in October and November, partly because Marlene had found work as a bookkeeper at a resort in Rancho Mirage. She told me, "My job will terminate in May. We can resume our travel schedule then."

Shortly after her new job began, I became puzzled about some of Marlene's actions. She renewed her weekend visits to the Los Angeles philanthropist, Wallace Weller, for whom she performed personal accounting. "I need the money," she said. "You know that Wallace pays me $400 for each visit."

I was content to give her all the free reins she needed. Marlene took this literally, and began riding more frequently at the polo grounds. Even this, however, did not lift her out of the doldrums.

Marlene's new job was 45 minutes away, so we generally would not see each other until we dined late at night. Special events kept coming up for her at the resort, or one place or another, so she often had to cancel our plans. For my part, I was preoccupied by professional engagements and many other projects. I assumed this was just a stage with Marlene, but that we would pass through it.

Early on, Marlene had asked me to write down what I considered most important in preserving a healthy relationship. "Open communication and patient understanding," I said. More and more, Marlene wrote nagging notes—and then refuted them with "Love you always" messages. I pleaded with her to get everything off her chest by talking to me, but to no avail.

Accepting Marlene's preference for written communication, I composed some questions for her later that fall. Her replies were succinct:

• *Do you tend to withdraw and refuse to talk about important issues?*
  "No," she wrote.

- *Do I ever disregard what you say or put you down?*
  "No."
- *Do you dwell at all on what it would be like to be with someone else?*
  "No."
- *Does our relationship take a back seat to any of your other interests?*
  "No."
- *Does the thought of being with me years from now disturb you?*
  "No."

In December, I asked Marlene to list all the ways in which I made her feel good, and all the ways in which I made her feel bad. Her reply again was terse and direct: "Only if you do the same for me!"

I asked her why she was so hesitant to show me her financial accounts in keeping with the *Living Together Contract*. I also asked her to give me an emergency phone number when she traveled to Los Angeles. Marlene cheerfully offered to give me this information, but never did.

I wondered if she had become less patient because of my protracted divorce, or perhaps because the Secret Service had failed to bring Luis to justice. Marlene did not explain her moodiness.

I didn't mind her making suggestions about home improvements and new clothes for me, but when she submitted a long Christmas wish list before Thanksgiving, I thought it was somewhat presumptuous. Again she displayed a picture of a new ring she would like, one that would serve as a wedding ring as well as an engagement ring. The wish list included many clothes items and horse gear.

Marlene kept emphasizing how she had already purchased eight gifts for me, suggesting I do my Christmas shopping early. This did motivate me to shop earlier than usual, but she was clearly not pleased with my establishing a budget of $2,000.

"Marlene, the best things in life are free," I reminded her.

"Yes, they're *presents*," she replied with a wink.

Even when she was making a sharp point, Marlene could always defuse the situation with humor.

As it turned out, we were both happy on Christmas Eve with the other's thoughtfulness. "I really love the diamond ring—but all my gifts were really swell," wrote Marlene in an upbeat thank-you note. "Wow, what a Santa you are!"

On New Years Eve I toasted the arrival of 1993. "To our travels, and to our continued life together," I said, raising my glass to hers. I again felt very close to Marlene. It had been a momentous year, my new book was in press, and I felt on top of the world. Most important, I was living with the woman I loved.

In January, Marlene wrote that she would like to change our cohabitation agreement for 1993. The key change she wanted to make was to remain at my home "in case Brad expires before I do." To me this was off the wall. I took no action on the request, partly because Marlene never offered to discuss it with me.

When I had to use her phone in an emergency in January, I was sharply reprimanded. "Never touch my phone," she admonished. Her combination telephone-answering machine was sacred to her. I assumed that her abruptness merely reflected her private nature.

Unexpectedly, Marlene renewed talk of Lucille and my divorce problems. She peppered me with questions about the pending legal proceedings. Soon after, Marlene admitted to having frequent nightmares, and dealing with a lot of guilt.

Guilt? I assumed it must be related to Marlene's "pondering the Luis mess day and night." She avoided discussion of the subject.

Suddenly, Marlene began to avoid cuddling after making love. I thought of all the notes she used to leave, thanking me for the "Great sack-attacks" in the early morning hours. Now she complained she needed more sleep.

My feelings shifted from "It's too good to be true—it couldn't get better" to "Whoa, let's take stock and see where we're going." For Marlene, her expressions of love had gone from "I promise to honor, cherish and obey you now and always, and provide you with all the Great Sex you desire for the rest of our days" to "With my impatient and opinionated ways I hope you never take my bad habits personally."

I was blinded by my love. How could I kick this relationship back into high gear?

CHAPTER 8

▼

GREMLINS AND DEMONS

In February 1993, my divorce from Lucille was finalized. In the process, Lucille had lost two judgments and was bitter.

Our celebration was muted at best. Although the subject of remarriage was on my mind, it was not openly discussed. Communication with Marlene was in a state of suspense. The two of us needed to reevaluate our relationship before moving on.

Marlene's tastes seemed to be changing. Over dinner, she no longer took an interest in reviewing the day's events. She no longer cared for golf, or accepted my invitations to take trail rides at a nearby stable. She had been a fan of classical music, but now I noticed her dozing at orchestral concerts. At home, she played more country music and soft rock. Marlene stopped watching the news, preferring youth-oriented music videos and fantasy movies. Earlier, she had told me these were Luis's preferences, not hers.

What was happening? Marlene's favorite rhythms, day or night, remained those of the bedroom. It was easy for me to believe she was keeping her chastity pledge—but had Marlene simply dropped the pretense that we had other interests in common?

Once again, I deferred to Marlene's preference for written communication. This time, rather than leaving a letter for Marlene, I decided to read aloud something I had written, hoping it would spur discussion. My brief treatise was called *The Importance of Truth*. A portion:

"Love dies in an atmosphere of not receiving the complete truth...One thing we had always agreed upon was to be above-board about everything...If you don't tell the truth about your inner feelings, the resentment builds up...When you can't live up to a promise or commitment, discuss it, don't hide it..."

"So, what do you think?" I asked her.

"That was very well written," Marlene said.

Nothing more. I had hoped Marlene would be in a mood to talk, but she clearly wasn't. A few questions of mine were appended. She agreed to look at them, and answer in writing.

"Are you still as much in love with me?" I asked.

"Yes," answered Marlene.

This was reassuring. What bothered me, however, were some unaccountable accusations in her reply.

"You are a Halcion addict," Marlene had written. "You are too controlling of me. You ask too many questions."

A Halcion addict? I had seen three respected doctors, each of whom had approved my taking one pill per night. Just the month before, my family doctor recommended I continue as usual. What was Marlene talking about?

As for controlling Marlene, or questioning her, I had scrupulously avoided any intrusion into her private life. I wrote a note asking for her to give me examples, so that I could correct my behavior.

She did not answer. But to my surprise, she delighted me with the most beautiful greeting card I had ever received: "TO THE MOST WON-DERFUL MAN IN THE WORLD," it read. It included a note declaring how much she loved me.

In her postscript, Marlene added that I was "near perfect."

I kept this card on the kitchen island for a few days. Just when my financial consultant was to arrive, "The gremlins got it!" I never saw the card again.

During February, a minor incident occurred at the resort clubhouse where Marlene worked, an incident that should have piqued my atten-tion. Greeting Marlene at the entrance of the large dining room where we were about to sit down for dinner, I started to give her a customary hug. But as I approached her and opened my arms, she furtively glanced inside and simultaneously drew away. In lieu of a welcome, Marlene was saying "not in public here." The message didn't register that there was someone else in the room, and in her life.

Marlene now needed almost twice as much sleep at night as I did. Increasingly, she awoke at the slightest stirring. The distant rumble of thunder, and the weak vibrations of earthquakes, would awaken her with-out disturbing me. Even the gentle rustling of the palm trees interfered with her sleep, and she kept thinking the noises came from rats in the attic.

A small confrontation triggered what I later viewed as the beginning of the end. We had just returned home from a lavish charity benefit, and as we walked through the kitchen, I answered a business call. I told Marlene I would take it in my study.

Rather than hang up the kitchen phone, Marlene remained silently on the line.

I questioned her afterwards about this, telling her it reminded me of a phone call that she had secretly recorded on her home phone a year before. I had discovered the tape soon after Marlene unpacked her belongings the previous June. She had left the tape in my computer room, where she probably planned to erase it on my transcribing system. I had assumed the mini-cassette to be my own, and started to use it in my tape-recorder to dictate some letters.

"Are my ears deceiving me?"

My dismay increased as I played the conversation again and again. I remembered the call so well. Shortly after telling Lucille in Florida that I was divorcing her, I phoned Marlene. It struck me as odd that she would ask so many questions about Lucille, as she already knew the answers.

The potential significance of the recording dawned on me: Marlene could have used the tape as blackmail in the event I reconciled with Lucille. She had recorded the conversation without my knowledge or consent.

That previous June, I had summoned Marlene to my study, and played the tape for her while looking her in the eye. Marlene was dumbstruck.

"How did you get hold of my tape? You took it from my answering machine."

After studying her intense but emotionless expression, I dismissed the subject. Very little damage had been done, I reasoned, and there was no certainty that she had actually recorded the conversation for illegitimate purposes. Marlene had this uncanny ability to push the right buttons.

As I dropped the tape into the wastepaper basket in front of me, I said quietly, "Let's drop it here."

Nearly nine months had passed, and nothing more had been said. Now Marlene had been caught eavesdropping on a private business exchange. At first, she acted as if I was fabricating the charge. Then she retreated in a huff, returning later to ask whether I had destroyed the infamous tape.

"It went out with the garbage, as far as I know."

When I entered the kitchen the next morning, I found a poison-pen letter from Marlene:

"I have searched my mind, and I can only figure this: you stole that tape out of my machine, as I never replace any tapes. You never told me, as that way you would have had to admit your stealing. Nice try, but no cigar! You are too nosy…it was of course self-explanatory how it got taped, since the machine was

on record mode…had I heard of this before, I never would have moved in
with you.”

I could have walked away from this acid diatribe and let the situation
die, but I chose to face it head-on. Trust issues were the chief reason I had
earlier broken up with Marlene. What really made an impact on her was
that I had made a summary of the taping incident the year before, and had
kept a copy in my safe deposit box. A few days later, I provided the
account, accompanied by a friendly note with a loving close.

She wrote the following on the bottom of my note:

*"Hello, Lover—AKA the Halcion Kid. I'll make you a deal. You stop the
multitude of questions, and I won't leave you any irate notes. Okay?"*

Stalemate. Marlene retreated into the bedroom for several days, claim-
ing illness. Marlene was feeling so poorly that I wrote a consoling letter,
suggesting that she might reduce her "bundle of nerves" by slowing down
and relaxing more. I offered additional assistance in household chores, and
encouraged her to widen her interests.

For several months, Marlene and I had no longer gone biking together
in the morning. I, however, remained as passionate as ever about exercising. Who could not love the brilliant morning sky, the golden hues on the
sharply silhouetted desert mountains? As March began, and the wildflowers burst into bloom, I taped a short memoir for my grandchildren on my
bike ride. It was titled *The Grandeur of March in the Desert.*

I showed the essay to Marlene, who read it without apparent interest.
What had happened to her? She no longer shared my joy in living in the
desert. Was she indifferent to the brilliance of nature, to the wildflowers
bursting into color? Here was a woman who loved Van Gogh and Monet
and had covered the walls with fine framed reproductions. Earlier,
Marlene could not get enough of nature; now Marlene's vacant green eyes
emitted no spark of enthusiasm.

Marlene's stoical mask had become impossible to decipher. I was living
with a stranger.

In March, I overheard Marlene explode in frustration while trying to understand one of our new computer money-management programs. On a card to me the next morning, she wrote:

"I may get impatient and upset at times, but it's only a momentary thing and never alters the way I feel deep down inside. You are the best. I love you."

Nevertheless, her nagging notes increased in frequency, despite a promise to stop writing them. They were her only form of maintaining control. She said, "When I get upset or ticked off, I take pen to paper and put down how and what I feel at the moment."

Marlene invariably found fault with the way I was acting in the household, but closed each complaint with a honey-tongued "I love you." I began to wonder how she could be so soothing in one phrase and in the next moment so caustic.

"My colitis flares and I have recurring headaches, insomnia and diarrhea," she said in another note. She also complained of a chronic sore throat, as well as an aching back and legs. When not hiding in the bedroom, however, Marlene was spending even more time at the polo grounds, at the theater, or in Los Angeles. She babysat for a friend, and was handling even more parties at the clubhouse.

I expressed concern for her health. "Don't worry," she said. "I'm trying different chiropractors and a good massage therapist."

Marlene still indulged in good humor. I even laughed when she told me in the bedroom, "I'm only doing this for charity."

It was true, our intimacy was beginning to suffer. What could I do to change it? How could I solve the problem?

*   *   *

As the middle of March approached, Marlene began to leave even more cryptic messages.

March 10, 1993: *"Thanks for your patience, for just being there when I'm grumpy, and frazzled, and mean as a bear."*

March 11, 1993: *"Sorry that I act the way I do, but I suffer many Demons and from constant headaches. Let's have a session after dinner."*

Marlene, the native German speaker who had lost her spoken accent, had a peculiar habit of capitalizing nouns in her sentences.

"Demons," Marlene had written. Marlene suffered from Demons.

*　　　　*　　　　*

On March 12, 1993, I left an article for Marlene on desert wildflowers, a subject which had once inspired her. I also left a newspaper clipping about Steve Allen and Dinah Shore, who were to be featured in a Desert Charities show. I asked her whether I should purchase tickets.

That same day, Marlene told me she was going to see a new chiropractor at 4:00 p.m., and wouldn't be home until after 7:00 p.m. We hardly exchanged any words, except a passing comment about the Saint Patrick's Day party at Davnet Duggan's home the next evening.

In truth, I had no inkling of what was to happen. When I looked at Marlene, I could see only innocence. Yes, it was true that Marlene, this most beautiful wildflower, was just beginning to drop her petals. Yet I was still too blinded by love to see anything grave in the situation.

During this period I thought back to my marriage with Linda. Other than my parents and two brothers, Linda had been the most moral person I had ever known. Because of Linda, I saw love and romance through a rose-colored prism.

I desperately wished I could feel the same way about Marlene.

CHAPTER 9

MEDICAL EMERGENCY!

The paramedics, who arrived at Casa del Vista on Saturday, March 13, shortly after 4:45 p.m., found I had been transferred from the toilet onto the nearby bed. I had been unconscious for two hours.

"My fiancé probably confused his Halcion with his Vitamin C, which he pops so much," Marlene explained. By her account, the Halcion vial had been tipped over, with four remaining pills spilled beside it. She showed the paramedics my Vitamin C bottle on the bathroom vanity nearby. Of course she avoided comparing its large white tablets with the tiny blue sleeping pills.

Both Marlene and I were health and fitness-minded. We exercised, watched our diets carefully, and used vitamin supplements. Because the Vitamin C seemed to ward off heavy colds, I took ten to twelve of the 1000 mg tablets per day. However, I never took more than two Vitamin C tablets at a time, and always from the bottle kept in the kitchen.

It was obvious that Marlene had staged the bathroom scene and placed the Vitamin C beside the Halcion. Why would I take a handful of Halcion, when my doctor had prescribed one pill at bedtime?

Most of my life I had been free of insomnia, and skeptical of sleep remedies. After my chemotherapy, however, my body chemistry changed. Although I had no difficulty going to sleep at night, I would rouse every hour or so, feeling wide awake. Once I started taking Halcion, I discovered that if I neglected to take one before retiring, my sleep would again be interrupted.

As the ambulance sped toward the hospital, I responded "in very slow slurred speech" to several questions posed by the paramedics. Apparently this is a rather common phenomenon for patients en route to the hospital, particularly those who have received overdoses or had seizures.

"Mr. Dunaway, can you hear us?"

"Yes," I said.

"Did you take Halcion?" they asked.

"No," I said.

According to the paramedics report, I even told them that I wanted to be sure to get back for the Saint Patrick's Day party that night. Despite a probable overdose, the paramedics concluded that I had probably not attempted suicide.

"Several possibilities have been entertained, including Halcion effect or overdosage…" This was recorded in my "Impression at Admission" report. An emergency nurse recorded what had been told to her by the paramedics. "Halcion vial 10 pills short, 4 tablets left."

Despite the notes, the emergency room doctor ordered no quantitative or other test for the drug. Only a general toxic screen was performed.

When questioned afterward, the attending physician replied defensively: "I had no reason to suspect poisoning."

Consulting doctors raised their eyebrows when they heard about this doctor's response and his inappropriate decisions in the emergency room.

Privately, I wondered what the autopsy and forensic pathologist would have said had I *not* pulled through, particularly in light of the doctor's negligence.

When my Day-Timer for February was checked, I discovered a notation that I had made when the monthly Halcion prescription was filled: "2 pills left." My overdose must have been 12 pills, not ten. And who knew whether Marlene had saved pills from previous months?

Research showed that eight pills alone could bring about a seizure, even in a young person. Twelve pills, totaling 3.0 mgs, was considered "a lethal poisoning overdose" for someone my age.

Before I left the hospital that Sunday, a different doctor had taken the floor. He assured me that quantitative tests would be run immediately from my original blood and urine samples. Nevertheless, testing was postponed time and time again by the hospital, and it would take more than a month before an independent laboratory undertook a quantitative analysis on the blood sample. Although Halcion is quick to break down, the rate of this decay allows the specialist to calculate the amount of the drug ingested originally. The independent report concluded that "a high quantity of Halcion had been absorbed on the date of the incident." I had my answer.

It was no small miracle that I survived, and that I suffered no apparent after-effects. Immediately, I became convinced that I must investigate on my own to better understand the full truth about Marlene. With care and diligence, I began to document everything that had occurred both before and after March 13, 1993.

CHAPTER 10

▼

AFTERMATH

"Hon, I think you'd better see your doctor about this," said Marlene.

She was standing in the kitchen, holding the Halcion vial in her hand. A look of concern played across her face. It was an expression I had seen countless times before over the course of our nine months living together.

"Hon?"

"I'll be seeing the doctor tomorrow," I grumbled.

It was Sunday evening. I had been poisoned the previous afternoon, and released from the hospital just that morning. Now Marlene was trying some spin control. She was coyly suggesting that an accident, or an addiction, might be responsible for what had happened.

I couldn't forget the three hours I waited to be picked up at the hospital. Furthermore, Marlene had pleaded with the staff to keep me hospitalized several more days. Marlene's behavior was unconscionable. Now I wondered what damage she had done in my absence.

Marlene was desperate to win me back. I had come home to find a Hallmark card with a note: "Thank you for always showing me you care!"

The two of us were quickly in a stand-off situation, but by noon, Marlene left a second card: "I love you more each day!" she had added.

A third card came later that day: "I'm sorry you had a mishap. These things really scare *me*. What the cause was really does not matter now. What matters is that you are A-OK!"

Marlene purchased greeting cards in large batches, and always seemed to have one for the appropriate occasion or sentiment. She showered them with such subtlety and finesse that I never noticed she carried such a complete supply.

Now her notes and cards were coming at a frantic, feverish pitch. Before leaving for work the next morning, Marlene had left a fourth card:

"Hon, have a great day and I hope you're back to the good old Brad again! The one that is kind and sweet. Luv you!"

*   *   *

When I was diagnosed with cancer in 1990, I believed it was the gravest danger I would ever face. Little did I suspect that lurking in my own household was a menace even more subtle and dangerous: an *evil mind*.

Sunday afternoon I was already securing medical records and reconstructing the chain of events. Secretly, I began to interview hospital personnel. On my way home, I stopped at the fire station and upon encountering a deputy sheriff, reported the poisoning. He agreed to hold the information in a suspense file.

After Marlene left for work Monday morning, I phoned my attorney. As luck would have it, he had recently reviewed our *Living Together Contract* and the 30-day notice of separation.

"Get her out of the house right away," he warned.

"I'll certainly do that as soon as possible," I replied.

"Do it now," he said. "Immediately!"

I didn't dare allow Marlene to stay in my home any longer than absolutely necessary, but this was a pivotal time and I wanted to play it safe. What items had she taken while I was hospitalized? It was obvious she had gone through my files and removed documents.

What financial damage had been done? I needed to check all of my accounts. And especially, I needed Marlene's list of belongings before she walked away with my treasure trove of possessions.

Monday evening, when Marlene came home and gave me a conciliatory bear hug, I remarked to myself how hollow and empty the gesture felt. This must have been the way Marlene felt the whole time. How could anyone who loved a person attempt to poison him?

Nobody thinks of being murdered in real life. That was something for books, movies, or television. Even so, I had little chance to analyze Marlene's motives. I was too busy going through records and dealing with doctors and hospitals.

Marlene seemed pleased I had done the grocery shopping that day. Attempting to be helpful, she asked me to prepare a "Things To Do" list for her. I was only too happy to comply.

Late that night, I canceled the credit card that Marlene was using. Acting on a hunch, I called my other credit card companies while Marlene slept and discovered that she had been charging without my knowledge. What could I do to protect my financial status, and how had Marlene undermined me already? She was a bold bookkeeper.

I discovered that the amount Marlene owed me had grown to over $5,000. She soon knew that I wanted a full account of her debts to me, as well as a record of household expenditures. In truth, I was most concerned about what Marlene had already removed. Pages were missing from my diary, and files were misplaced or taken away.

Three nightmarish days followed. I made certain that I went to bed after Marlene and that I rose before her. Taking every possible precaution, I arranged to eat out or pick up my food at restaurants. I was still absorbed in disbelief, checking my perceptions against grim reality.

Marlene put on her most happy-go-lucky face. She was a remarkable actress, I thought. No longer did she complain about her aches and chronic illnesses. They had apparently faded overnight. Fortunately, she returned late from work and only once did she try to lure me to the bedroom.

"Make my evening," she enticed me, parodying Clint Eastwood, her erstwhile friend.

By Thursday night, Marlene seemed frayed at the edges. I had all but demanded that she sit down and work out her math. After Marlene had made a halfhearted attempt to bring the financial records current, I prepared an eviction order in the early hours of the morning:

"*My attorney reviewed our Living Together Contract…and has recommended that I inform you that, under the circumstances that prevail, you will no longer be welcome at Casa del Vista following your departure during the morning hours of March 19. You are given 30 days to remove your belongings…*"

I left the note in the kitchen and planned to be there in the morning to answer questions. When I reached the kitchen about 7:00 A.M., a note from Marlene was already on the table.

She wrote, "I hope you're satisfied *now*!—if I am still alive by then [April]. I won't be going to the brunch with our friends. Just tell them I am *dead*. Might be true by *then*."

Marlene spent a few minutes gathering some belongings, and told me that she would be back Monday evening to take more. On leaving, she left another note:

"Thank you so much for your kind concern and lovely notice—all of which is and was most FORESEEN!"

I followed Marlene to her car and watched as she entered.

"You never loved me!" she said.

"I loved you more than I've loved anybody else." And *I* meant it.

*   *   *

Marlene phoned from work on Sunday and left a disquieting message:

"I know you're snooping through my things, and I'm going to call the police if you don't phone immediately!"

After I responded late Sunday afternoon, Marlene removed some of her personal effects that night. Upon leaving she said, "We are just not compatible."

It took Marlene, Everett and his girlfriend six trips to move everything. Although the list of personal possessions had been prepared for me, I doubted she would abide by it. Consequently, I tried to arrange for my trusted housekeeper to be on the scene when they arrived. She was shocked by the language Marlene used when she saw I had hired an observer.

"Will you be here this Saturday?" Marlene asked my housekeeper.

"I'll be away," she said.

Naturally, Marlene scheduled her heaviest moving for the housekeeper's day off. That Saturday, I asked about my missing tools. Marlene showered me with obscenities and, seething with anger, threw a screwdriver in my direction.

"Screw yourself," she shouted.

These were the first foul-mouthed utterances I had heard from her and the first conspicuous loss of control. Was this the real Marlene Hirsch Washington on display?

The three movers and shakers—with emphasis on shakers—fanned out into different parts of Casa del Vista. I didn't dare raise my voice, fearing this might incite their pack mentality. Although increasingly uncomfortable with their contempt and with their high-handed disregard for my property, I let them take items not on the list. The stolen belongings even included some of my fixtures.

I reminded Marlene that after peeling the entry sticker from her car window, there could be no further entry through the security gate. She replied, "I have other friends in the area and can come though the gate any time I want to." It was an ominous warning, although I could not begin to know its implications.

Before Marlene left for the last time, she placed a copy of a "Pluses and Minuses for Brad" list where my housekeeper would most likely find it. "Pluses" included good sex and a sense of humor. "Minuses" included my so-called addiction.

I reflected on my experiences with Marlene, and counted my blessings that I had not allowed her to become my cancer caretaker three years earlier. The emotions evoked by me after the poisoning were revulsion, repulsion and resignation. The dreams were gone. But I didn't feel anguish or suffering, nor did I feel sympathy or pity. It wasn't as though the sun stopped shining, rather that a new source of light had been cast. What had once been an aura of peace and harmony had become feelings of goodbye and good riddance. This was truly a case of betrayal far beyond forgiveness.

Did I still love Marlene to the extent that I harbored any feelings of wanting to see her any time in the future? The answer was NO. It was not as if I had lost a loved one by death and was in mourning. Nor was it like losing a loved one by his or her leaving. There were no tears.

With the act of poisoning, she had violated the most basic principle of human rights, which is the right to live. Nevertheless, because of the memorable nine months together, I did not regret meeting and knowing Marlene. After all, if it hadn't been for Marlene and the poisoning, there wouldn't have been this continuing saga.

I recalled the precept to be cautious about anything that seems too good to be true. And I remembered one of Marlene's favorite songs, *How to Handle a Woman*. The final refrain goes, "The way to handle a woman, is to love her, simply love her, merely love her, love her, just love her."

I felt I had done the best I could. "It's been grand knowing you…It's been fun, it's been grand."

CHAPTER 11

▼

THE INVESTIGATION

The day after Marlene was evicted from Casa del Vista, I had done enough checking of my files and trash cans to know that a professional investigator was needed. That Saturday night I selected the name of Warren Stellar from the Yellow Pages, and arranged to have Stellar meet me at home the next morning.

Although I read that Stellar had almost 40 years of investigative experience, only later would the breadth and range of the detective's skill be fully realized.

Credentials reviewed and formalities aside, I explained the poisoning, and how in good conscience I could not enter Marlene's bedroom and look at her private files. I had no idea what records she had, or where. Warren Stellar immediately swung into action. While I retired to my study, Stellar spent two hours taking notes from a large number of documents which he was able to inspect and replace without a trace of his being in our master bedroom.

This was the beginning of a long investigation. Through the private gate of PGA West, with ever-tightening security, poured a succession of investigators and informants.

Warren Stellar was a renowned private eye, one of the best in the business. He had retired as Chief Investigator for the District Attorney's office of Santa Barbara County. Two of his specialties were teaching criminal investigation and handling mediation in divorce cases. Stellar's broad education in police science and administration of justice served him well when he opened his own detective agency in 1983. His record as a detective appeared to be spotless, unlike the notorious sleazy or flamboyant P.I.'s of movies and television.

Stellar proved to be meticulous and resourceful at every turn. As an employee, he was unfailingly ethical. He was a better actor than many of the TV and movie stars he represented. Stellar could custom-disguise his voice, and change his appearance and vehicles to fit any situation. He staged elaborate theatrical traps to obtain new information.

One of his notable masquerades was sprung on Marlene's ex-husband whom he phoned in Florida.

"Mr. Washington," he began, "I'm with Search International, a group that makes special searches for possible heirs. I'm trying to ascertain if you ever lived in California." The ex-husband accepted the bait and recited his Navy experience in California.

"Were you ever married?"

"Oh, yeah. I was married twice. First to Judy and then to Marlene."

"No kidding! I was married twice, too. Did you get married again?"

"No. I'm single now. Being married is too much trouble."

"I know what you mean," he laughed. "Do you have any children?"

"Oh, yes." Washington told him about his two children with Judy.

"Are you still in the Navy?"

"No, I'm retired." Then, Washington became even more talkative, describing his retirement and recent work in computers.

Stellar continued, "Well, the only thing that doesn't check out is that this deceased person is black."

"Oh, *I'm* black!"

And the detective had all the information he needed.

Stellar could make an emotional connection to total strangers. His gift of gab invariably charmed his subjects, and drew out deeper insights into Marlene's character and actions. Few, if any, of the people Stellar met had any idea they were talking to a detective.

To find out more about Everett, for example, Stellar posed as a prospective homebuyer. Stellar paid a visit to the mother of Everett's girlfriend, and even brought his own wife along to make his interest seem credible. Through the cracks in the conversation, Stellar found out a great deal about Everett and his girlfriend's family.

On leaving the house, Stellar asked about the lot line near where Everett's pick-up truck was parked. Jokingly, he said, "How about throwing in that good looking truck with the deal?"

"Oh, no, that belongs to my daughter," she laughed.

Another mystery was solved. Everett had access to vehicles that did not belong to him, and sometimes used them to abet his mother's schemes.

On another occasion, Stellar needed to confirm the number of Marlene's condominium unit within a gated complex. He took his stepdaughter with him as driver and delivery girl. As rehearsed, she pulled up to the unmanned front gate and pressed the intercom button for the name Washington.

"Yes?" Marlene's voice answered.

"Miss Washington, I'm delivering flowers from the Bouquet Florist. What is your unit number?"

"Oh, thank you. Come right to number 20." Marlene gave directions and the gate buzzed open. Their mission accomplished, they made a U-turn and left Marlene waiting, a bit perplexed.

The detective's ventures on my behalf were as ingenious as the best out of a spy novel. Once he caught a scent, he'd sniff out the target, phone me and write a follow-up report. His targets became easy marks for him. They'd open up and tell tales that ordinarily would never have been revealed. No one seemed to foil him.

Warren Stellar rarely returned empty-handed from any of his quests, particularly to courthouses and to city and county seats. With the help of his many Internet contacts, he quickly amassed a burgeoning file on Marlene. He coordinated parts of his work with one of the two genealogists I hired.

Stellar uncovered Marlene's records related to her State Workers Compensation Claim. After termination by Dr. Randolph, she had answered an advertisement placed by a psychological firm that specialized in disability damages. The firm filed claims on her behalf for Workers Compensation against Dr. Randolph, citing impaired work functions and severe mental depression.

Warren Stellar produced copies of reports by two psychologists, including accounts of her therapy sessions during the first six months of 1992. These were sensitive and revealing private documents.

Stellar seemed to receive feedback unavailable to other investigators, and he always reported back to me promptly. His waggish report titles soon changed to "The Black Widow Hooker."

I hadn't realized Stellar had made a science of "garbology" until I mentioned to him some interesting information that I discovered when combing through my trash. Marlene had stayed in close touch with a male friend over the years. Garbology revealed that she wrote him in February 1993 about her plans to terminate our relationship. This was a total surprise to me, as February was a month of some of her most amorous advances.

It was also discovered that Marlene began spreading word that I had been trying to take from her the $150,000 settlement that she still sought from the breast surgeon. She claimed my "con artist scheme" became apparent early in 1993, but had evolved before she moved in with me. "He's a cheapskate and was seeking a lady with money." This sounded like a repeat of Marlene's story that her ex-husband "was just interested in my money."

One of the most remembered of Stellar's achievements occurred the day of my only meeting with Marlene after she moved from Casa del Vista. Marlene phoned me on April 23, asking to see me at Cactus Pete's Restaurant that afternoon. She wanted to negotiate some of her debts.

"I'll meet you at 4:30 P.M.," she said, "since I have a dinner date at 6:30." Having no idea what to expect, I left a message for Stellar, telling him the time and place of the meeting. Marlene and I both arrived at 4:30 and finished 35 minutes later.

Our discussion was business-like and civil, and we came to an agreement without difficulty. At the close of the meeting, Marlene began to question me. She wondered about the possibility of my reuniting with Lucille. I didn't suspect that she had already contacted and met with Lucille. Nor did I understand the expression on Marlene's face when I informed her that the Secret Service now knew of Luis's whereabouts. She asked if I had been in contact with any of her friends and requested that I not talk to any of them. What did all of this mean?

As Marlene rose from the table, I took the opportunity to return her compliments on the "Pluses" list she had prepared for me before she moved out. "That was a wonderful nine months, Marlene," I said matter-of-factly. Her startled look is still etched in my memory. The poisoning would never be forgiven by me, but I was not about to deny the nine months of happiness I had experienced living with her.

When Marlene left the parking lot, I looked around for Stellar but didn't see him. He probably didn't get the message, I thought.

About 8:30 P.M. Stellar phoned me. The detective had not only observed our meeting and photographed it, but had followed Marlene to her next destination: a resort country club in a distant part of the desert. Stellar, switching his surveillance vehicle and changing his clothes, had observed Marlene's car in the carport of a duplex condo overlooking a greenbelt.

Behind the greenbelt he found a hidden vantage point and took telephoto images of Marlene dining on the patio with an elderly gentleman.

In the days following, Stellar developed a detailed profile on this gentleman, who turned out to be the part-owner of her sports car purchased in 1991.

One evening shortly thereafter, Stellar followed Marlene on her way to a rendezvous with another date whom she had met only three weeks before. This time Marlene apparently sensed she was being followed. She went in one door of several closely grouped restaurants, and out another door, before driving her typical route with many shortcuts and quick turns. My detective wished he had one of his companion trail cars to leapfrog ahead and lessen suspicion. It was a game of cat and rat, but the clever cat was not about to be foiled.

Stellar managed to follow her through the tightly guarded gates of a distant resort, and caught up with her just as the garage door swung down to hide her vehicle. In a mere three weeks, Marlene had already acquired an automatic garage-door opener to her lover's residence.

This well-known 72-year-old gentleman was a recent widower and a French Canadian who remained extremely active. Marlene once again had three or four Sugar Daddies, not to mention some casual liaisons at the polo grounds. Her love life had clearly not missed a beat after leaving my home.

Immediately after her eviction, Marlene lived briefly with her pudgy Italian friend, Nick Celani. Through Marlene, he had earlier expressed an interest in purchasing an RV that I had inherited. Celani phoned me about the RV after Marlene's eviction, and left a message on my answering machine: "…also I've been trying to get hold of, oh-uh, what's her name, and her line's dead…I wonder what's happening."

I had to chuckle over the absurdity of that little charade, knowing that Marlene was probably cuddling with Celani at the time of his call. "A typical con artist tactic," noted Warren Stellar. After a bit of investigation,

Celani proved to be a shady dealer. This was not the last time I was to hear from him.

       *   *   *

I suspected Marlene's co-conspirator was her son, particularly when I returned from the hospital and found his puppy at my home. My suspicions increased when the housekeeper told me that a guest room bed had been used while I was hospitalized.

Everett had behaved like a common thief during the removal of his mother's belongings, but his participation in planning the poisoning remained vague until an informer recorded Marlene's voice on tape. "Everett and I are trying to figure out some way to get rid of him," she said.

This threat was shocking to me, because my relationship with Everett had been friendly, although somewhat distant. It also surprised me when Marlene included Everett as a plaintiff on a Restraining Order she fabricated. It was not until much later that I more clearly understood Everett's wrath, although my denial of a job as my gardener had clearly upset him.

A full investigation of Everett by my investigation team, as well as a review of the records of Marlene's luncheon meetings with her son, were necessary before his role as co-conspirator became obvious.

While driving a motorcycle in San Francisco in November 1990, Everett had received a citation. Then in 1991 he was arrested for "throwing a lighted substance," and his license was suspended. Through 1993, Everett had not paid the bail, and therefore no longer owned a legitimate driver's license.

During the summer of 1993, as part of the investigation, a former narcotics agent tailed Everett and concluded that he was not only a drug user, but a *dealer*. The investigator saw him peddling, then trailed him to a known drug district.

"Two drug stops were made," he reported. "A pick-up was made from under the hood of a junk-heap of a car parked at a vacant house that was for sale. Everett had the lethargic and frail look of a drug addict. He invariably appeared to be in a stupor, wandering around, losing his way to places and driving like one under the influence." When drugs started controlling Everett, he started selling them so he could continue to buy them.

I now better understood Everett's slovenly appearance whenever he'd come to Casa del Vista. He seemed to have highs and lows, and both he and his girlfriend continually looked worn out or spacey.

Everett moved his living and working quarters even more frequently than his mother. Stellar tracked him from place to place as he tried to conceal his whereabouts. A Social Security trace showed he used friends' addresses as mail drops, and kept switching lodgings and vehicles. Marlene's girlfriend, Davnet, once commented to me that she wondered why he had such a difficult time landing jobs and holding them.

Stellar trailed Marlene in May 1993 to a small condominium near the polo grounds which she shared at first with Everett and his girlfriend. He found that Everett and Marlene continued to use the same joint bank account and rental mail box. Marlene routinely changed one digit in her Social Security, telephone and driver's license numbers.

It took over five years to investigate the labyrinth of rifts and chasms in Marlene's life, but a transient way of life now seemed second-nature. Marlene did all she could to thwart the investigation. She spread malicious stories that prevented some of her social and business contacts from talking to my investigators.

Warren Stellar persevered, and would in time complete a comprehensive account of Marlene's activities. "*I can see clearly now…*" as the soft popular tune goes. With all the information in place, we were at last ready to reconstruct the poisoning episode.

CHAPTER 12

▼

RECONSTRUCTION
OF THE POISONING

Why did Marlene choose to end our relationship by a murderous act?

Most certainly, it involved her lust for financial gain via promiscuity. She was bound and determined that in love, life or divorce, I'd pay as I left.

Trust issues had already been STRIKE ONE against her. If I found out about any of her ongoing liaisons, she knew that would be STRIKE TWO or THREE.

My consideration of marriage was on hold, and she realized it was not immediately forthcoming. Several weeks before the poisoning, she had typed a terse reminder: "You have NEVER asked me to marry you." Marlene wondered why I didn't propose marriage after my divorce from Lucille became final on February 1, 1993. After all, I had bought her a Christmas ring to serve eventually as a wedding ring.

How was the date of March 13 selected by Marlene for the poisoning? She had to pick a day she didn't work, because only then did she serve me soup for lunch. What better day to arrange this than a Saturday, the one day she usually prepared my lunch after she rode at the polo grounds? The Saturday of the Saint Patrick's Day party served her purpose best. It later became obvious that she hoped to go to the party *without* me to resume a recent flirtation with a priest.

The poison plot was hatched before December, because that month Marlene secretly intercepted from my mail the two new 1993 entrance stickers issued to PGA West homeowners. The stickers enabled co-conspirator Everett to enter the security gate without being stopped or detected.

Surreptitiously, Marlene and Everett concocted their plan, perhaps making some dry runs of the whole scheme while I was out of town. They wanted to make certain I would be absent when the soup was made, so they arranged for me to be at the polo grounds, ostensibly to take pictures of Marlene on her horse, "Queen."

After the poisoning, I checked on her horse's name, which was "Honey." There was no "Queen." Marlene had supplied a false name in the event I tried to locate the horse itself when she didn't show up for our photo session.

During my absence it would have been easy for the conspirators to take the 12 Halcion tablets from the bathroom, pulverize them, and dissolve them into the soup. I was unaware that my lunch had been doctored. The medication did not significantly change the flavor of the zesty vegetable soup that I devoured while talking about the Saint Patrick's Day party being held that night at Davnet's.

Marlene told an informant that she had napped for two hours after lunch as an outlet for her anxiety, "to escape from Brad's clutches," she said.

It is believed Marlene found me comatose on the toilet by 3:00 P.M. Discovering me there was a complete surprise. In fact, she admitted to searching most of the house before finally locating me. Her first move was probably to phone Everett, requesting his help in moving me from the toilet onto the bed where I was supposed to be taking a nap. A later reenactment of moving my dead weight from the toilet to the bed demonstrated that Marlene couldn't have done this alone. She claimed my bed was wet after I napped, probably not realizing that the bed became wet only after she and Everett dragged me from the commode with soggy pants.

Marlene made a strange phone call to the security gate as the ambulance approached the entrance. "This is Mrs. Dunaway. An ambulance is now arriving at the gate. Please let them through."

Security responded by opening the gate for the paramedics without screening a "mystery" third passenger, a female. She was observed hunched in the middle of the two front seats occupied by two male attendants. When queried at a later date, the ambulance company had no record of a third person in the ambulance. The only explanation of the mystery passenger was that she was Everett's girlfriend. Was this why Marlene sought to expedite entry?

Everett had been in training as a paramedic, and remained friendly with local paramedics. Marlene had told me, "He quit the training because he couldn't stand to see people dying."

Marlene and Everett probably kept checking my condition for over an hour, realizing that I was still breathing. Why didn't Brad die? Twelve tablets were more than enough to do the job! The conspirators must have been frantic and perhaps considered suffocation with a pillow, but that could be detected by an autopsy. They had to cover their tracks, because I would surely have a lot of questions if I survived. A new scenario had to be improvised.

Marlene felt compelled to call 9-1-1, and finally, at 4:37 P.M., she did. If she called any later, she knew I would wonder why she neglected to check on me at 4:00 P.M., the time she had suggested for lovemaking.

Marlene made the call from her private telephone in the master suite. If she had phoned when she found me in the bathroom at the other end of the residence, one would expect she'd call from that bedroom. This was another bit of evidence that some time had elapsed before the call was made.

Marlene told an informer on an authorized tape recording that she had discussed my condition with the dispatcher. "I told 9-1-1 that I had no way to know whether it was a seizure or what." The sheriff's tape of the call caught Marlene in another lie. She had merely told them I was asleep.

As I was being transferred to the ambulance, Marlene exited the garage in her white sports car in order to trail the paramedics. She had directed them to Desert Springs Hospital, which was not the preferred hospital that my doctors use. Although Marlene stated that she had called my family doctor whose phone number was at her fingertips, she never contacted him. And at no point did she inform my children!

When Marlene drove out of Casa del Vista, the young female patrol officer directing traffic clearly remembered "the blonde lady with the cold, expressionless face."

Ironically, Marlene *was* worried about me, fearful I might *not* die.

Everett remained at the house, now joined by his girlfriend. After the automatic sprinklers went on that evening, the large valve for the court-yard area was manually turned off so Everett's puppy wouldn't get soaked. He had to have done this, because Marlene was at the hospital. In addition, she wouldn't know where to find the remote water valve, nor did she have the strength to operate it.

Records at the Emergency Center showed that the "patient's wife went home prior to beginning of shift" at 7:30 P.M. This meant Marlene had left the hospital almost two hours before I was transferred, still unconscious, to the Intensive Care Unit. Marlene told an informer on tape that she left the hospital early that evening because her hypoglycemia required that she eat something every three to four hours. During the night, however, she made no inquiries about my condition.

By the time I returned Sunday from the hospital, my bedroom and bathroom were immaculate. Everything had been rearranged. The culprits had been busy through the night and early morning hours. It was obvious Marlene had gone through my belongings. She had pilfered my wallet and searched my diaries, removing selected pages. Items in my files were disarranged. Some files were missing altogether.

This probably explains, in part, why Marlene took three hours to make the short trip to the hospital to pick me up that Sunday morning. Upon reaching the hospital, she had pressured the doctor to keep me for two to three days of observation. I suspected she wanted more time to pore through my files at home, dispose of the pup, and formulate her alibis.

Marlene's accounts of the poisoning to medical personnel varied. In some accounts I was a Halcion addict, in others I swallowed the tablets accidentally, and in still others, I had planned the poisoning in order to frame her because I didn't love her anymore.

Davnet had been expecting us at her Saint Patrick's Day party Saturday night until Marlene phoned about 9:00 P.M. that I was in the hospital with a stroke. Immediately, the priest who was attending the party as Davnet's date offered to visit me early Sunday morning, even though he didn't know me. Marlene quashed this idea.

Marlene's attempt to poison me certainly comprised premeditation and malice aforethought. Today, I am still aghast that Marlene chose this route as her escape hatch.

I could only wonder what sort of youth had predisposed her to attempt first degree murder. What mysteries did her past hold? Who was this beautiful German bombshell?

CHAPTER 13

▼

MARLENE WHO?

Who *was* Marlene? After the poisoning, I was determined to find out all I could about her past. With the aid of Warren Stellar, two researchers, medical specialists and a host of informants, surprising secrets were revealed.

I flew to Germany, and with the help of an interpreter, began digging into Marlene's youth. We had little difficulty locating Fraus, Frauleins and Herrs with information about her. It soon became clear that many of her stories were distortions of the truth.

Marlene was the only child of Lutheran German parents, Karl and Elke Hirsch. Both were northern Germans who married in their late twenties. They lived in Bergedorf, a suburb east of Hamburg. While Marlene was still a baby, Karl went into the army and left for the Russian war front in 1941. He was captured by the Russians in 1942 and didn't return until 1948. Because of this, his daughter didn't really know him until she was eight years old.

"The German government declared my father officially dead. After a long absence, my mother married a British serviceman." Marlene had told the story many times. According to Marlene, her father's surprise return from the dead sent shock waves through the village.

Relatives told me this was not at all the case. Marlene's mother was actually well aware of Karl's whereabouts during his Russian years, and they corresponded with each other during his six-year incarceration. Elke Hirsch had not remarried in his absence.

Karl Hirsch had been held in a prison camp near the Caspian Sea, where he was pressed into hard labor in the underground mines. Suffering from malnutrition and exhaustion, he was of no further use to the Russians. He was sent home in 1948, just skin and bones. It took him years to recover his health and put on weight.

Before returning to Bergedorf, Karl sent Elke a telegram giving his train's arrival time. His wife was not there to greet him, and she didn't return until early the next morning. Elke had spent the night with a Polish serviceman she had met in Hamburg upon his release from a nearby prison camp about 1945.

It didn't take Karl long to realize that his pretty wife had been unfaithful for some time.

Elke was not the most devoted mother, either. Neighbors told how she left her infant daughter alone in the house. Marlene was once left on the veranda in her baby carriage. It grew late, the weather changed, and it was so cold that the infant actually turned blue. Neighbors brought her into their house, warming her over a gas stove.

Elke divorced Karl soon after his return to Bergedorf. In a German divorce, a guilty party must be decreed by the court. Elke was adjudged the guilty party.

She immediately married her Polish friend in order to leave Germany. Early in 1949, the two left for Canada to live in Kitchener, Ontario, where her husband's married brother had moved.

This was an emotional time for Marlene. She desperately wanted to accompany her mother, but her father had gained custody and desired she remain in Germany to attend a better school.

When speaking of her father, Marlene was always very critical. "He was extremely authoritarian—I didn't like him," she told me. In Germany, however, Karl Hirsch was consistently described as a kind and gentle man. We were shown photographs of him that reflected a sensitive nature. He was truly a devoted father who loved his daughter very much and wanted the best for her.

Karl did permit Marlene to move into the beautiful downtown apartment of her favorite aunt. She and her husband owned a bookstore in Bergedorf. According to relatives, they were extremely generous with their niece, and spoiled her. Moreover, the aunt sided with her sister in Canada and encouraged negativity toward Karl.

Marlene was a shy and somewhat unattractive teenager. She kept a personal journal through 1972, and in her diary recorded her perceived inadequacies. Marlene had attained her 5'5" stature at an early age, and was much taller and thinner than the other girls. She was bothered by a protruding nose, and later, by small, slow-to-develop breasts.

Marlene felt a longing for change. She greatly admired the German actress, Marlene Dietrich, and her liberated lifestyle. One day, Marlene Hirsch might also "charm the larks off the lilac trees" like her idol.

Elke frequently returned from Canada to Bergedorf. She and Marlene would laugh and play, and attend social functions together. Marlene recalled the wonderful times they shared, musing, "She was so much fun." Since she was quite young at the time, Marlene probably didn't know the true story about her mother. She was so devoted to Elke that she took her mother's side on any question involving Karl.

After less than a year in Canada, Elke found her second marriage unfulfilling. She re-registered in Germany in order to live there for a year. At that time, Marlene was ten years old, Elke 39, and Karl 41. Elke did her best to persuade Karl to re-marry her, but she was unsuccessful and eventually returned to Canada—again without Marlene.

In 1951, Karl married his second wife, Karin, who was a war widow. The couple would remain happily married for almost 40 years, until Karl's death at age 80. Karl worked in advertising and public relations with a Hamburg newspaper; Karin was employed nearby as a secretary. Both loved to hike and to keep trim and active.

Although Marlene liked her new stepmother, she never warmed to her father. "We'd take Marlene on vacation trips to Switzerland, but even on those trips, she was cold and harsh to her father and spoke only to me. Karl was terribly hurt. He would often say that Marlene not only looked like her mother but acted like her. He was so heartbroken with the poor relationship he had with his daughter that we decided not to have children," said Karin.

"Elke kept returning from Canada," Karin told me, "intent on obtaining custody. Marlene tried to persuade Karl to free her and allow her to go to Canada. Karl steadfastly refused while she was completing her schooling."

Marlene described her childhood as if she had been locked in an attic. "My father held me captive as revenge for my mother remarrying while he was imprisoned," she told me. Her bitterness toward her father appeared to increase with each unsuccessful appeal by her mother for custody.

Elke discovered she had breast cancer in 1952. When her condition worsened, she returned to Hamburg and re-registered in 1955. A full blood transfusion was performed in a futile attempt to stop the metastasis. Elke did not disclose her worsening condition to Marlene, however.

Appealing to Karl's sense of compassion, Elke persuaded Karl to allow Marlene passage to Canada at the end of the 1956 school year. Karl gave Elke the total amount of support he was supposed to pay until Marlene turned 18, and paid for her flights between Canada and Germany. Although Marlene was to continue her education in Canada, her formal schooling was complete at age 16 in Germany. Marlene later lied about completing an A.A. degree at age 19.

Whenever Marlene wrote her father from Canada, she would request money and include a list of things she wanted. Because Karin's salary went into a joint bank account with Karl, she was contributing to Marlene's support as well. "When Marlene asked for money, <u>we</u> would send her the money," she said.

One of Marlene's requests for money—$5,000 for furnishings in a newly acquired home—proved to be the last straw for her father. He politely replied, "No more."

In 1989 Karl had a heart attack and Marlene was notified that he might be dying. Karin and nurses at the hospital said he didn't look his age and thought he would recover. A day or so later he was quickly gone. His life had been serene with his second wife, but he was deeply saddened by the relationships with his first wife and his daughter.

Karl had prepared his Last Will in 1964. It was the usual type of will in Germany in which everything is left to the surviving spouse. After Karl died, Marlene contested the will, maintaining that a later one had been drawn up in 1967. In truth, there was no additional document or codicil.

Karin said, "I was terribly hurt when Marlene contested the will through the courts without first contacting me—so much so that I tore up all of my pictures of Marlene. I had to go to court to prove no additional will was made in 1967 when Marlene had come back here."

It was only when her father was on his deathbed that Marlene expressed a desire to see him again. Her attitude toward him apparently softened when a possible inheritance was at stake. She expected to inherit about $10,000. Marlene received nothing.

*   *   *

My visit to Germany convinced me that Canada might hold the key to a decade of Marlene's darkest roots. With the help of a German-French interpreter and candid relatives, I discovered why Marlene went to such considerable lengths to disguise her earlier life.

Kitchener, Ontario came as a profound cultural shock to the teenage girl. Living conditions were primitive, and adversity hung like a millstone around her mother's neck. Elke's husband, Ansel, was a mechanic who struggled to make ends meet. No wonder Elke wanted to leave Ansel and return to Germany. By contrast, Elke's German sister-in-law, Hilda, was content in Ontario with her young family.

"How could Elke bring 16-year-old Marlene back to Canada, when she knew that she was dying of breast cancer?" Hilda asked this question time and time again.

Less than three months after Marlene joined her mother, Elke died at age 44 in Kitchener. Her mother's death came suddenly, and Marlene mourned for a long time.

"Why did she have to die so soon?" she lamented. "I know I'm going to die young, too."

Although the relationship between Elke and her husband Ansel was often unhappy, Ansel did love his wife. Neighbors saw him crying for hours at her gravesite. For years he refused to look at other women, until Hilda encouraged him to write to a former girlfriend in Poland. When she came to Canada in 1960, they had not seen one another for 21 years. The two were soon married and had a son a year later.

Hilda spoke about her brother-in-law Ansel with affection, stressing what a gentle and simple man he was. "Elke was a city girl who liked the nice clothes, and who liked the nice life Marlene's father in Germany provided. Elke made Marlene who she was."

Marlene didn't like her stepfather, Ansel. Overcome with grief after Elke's death, Ansel asked Marlene to remain with him in his house. He tried to help her find work and even bought her a typewriter so that she might learn some basic secretarial skills. "Ansel tried to be good to Marlene, but she was so much like her mother: *spoiled*. Marlene would send to Germany pictures of dresses she wanted, and her aunt, a seamstress, would make the dresses exactly as she ordered."

Hilda suggested that Marlene go back to Germany and live with her aunt, but Marlene refused. "Ansel had custody, but he couldn't communicate with her. After she left him a few months later, he never heard from her again. Marlene had sought more money from him than he could give her. She learned from Elke to seek out men of means."

Marlene moved to the larger city of Hamilton, living with Hilda, her husband, Otto, and their 12-year-old son. "It was not an easy time for us," Hilda said. She was reluctant to say more.

Marlene claimed to me she lost her virginity in Hamilton to a "landlord/relative/friend" whom she lived with. "He raped me, but I offered no resistance. I let him do it." Was this man Otto, Hilda's husband? Later inquiries bore this out, and even revealed Marlene's subsequent blackmail attempts. It is likely that Otto, not Marlene, was the victim of this consensual "rape."

"Marlene is a person who may fall to the ground, but she lands on her feet like a cat," Hilda said.

Marlene moved to the lakefront city of Burlington, a part of the Golden Horseshoe that stretches between Hamilton and Toronto on the western shores of Lake Ontario. She took the position of dental nurse with Dr. Alexander, a man who remembered her well.

"Marlene fraudulently arranged to have a credit card issued in my wife's name," he related. "During a series of shopping sprees at Eatons [one of Canada's oldest and most prestigious department stores], she charged an exorbitant amount to Mrs. Alexander."

While the dentist was away on a ski trip, his wife opened the office mail before Marlene could intercept it. She discovered a range of spurious charges, all of the items purchased by Marlene for her own personal use. The dentist and his wife were so incensed they called their lawyer, who told them to report the fraud to the police. Marlene was charged and convicted.

Dr. Alexander said, "When I first found out about this, my dander was so worked up that I went to her apartment and gave her the bum's rush.

Marlene pleaded with me that she be allowed to continue working in my office.

"I was at her apartment twice, but was never invited inside. One time she came to the door and I was shocked to see her in high black leather boots." The thigh-high boots were a symbol of the sex sirens of the 60s, along with the mini-skirt introduced in 1965.

After reportedly serving a jail sentence, Marlene couldn't find a job. She was seen frequenting bars and working the streets in Hamilton as a prostitute while residing in a small downtown hotel.

How did her boyfriend, Steve, fit into the picture? Marlene referred to her Canadian years in terms of this charismatic English lover. "I met Steve in the 1960s. He was a playboy who had wealthy parents in England. We became very close, but he played around a lot."

Marlene's stepmother had referred to Steve as "Marlene's Englishman husband" and told me, "She took trips to England with him in 1964 and 1967 before flying on to Hamburg." Thus, their choppy relationship must have been rather lengthy, despite no record of marriage. Marlene did reveal on subsequent documents that Stephen Jeffries owed her $3,000 for child support.

Marlene told me about a daughter whom she had relinquished at a tender age. By refusing to discuss her child's whereabouts, she shrouded her in an aura of mystery. The daughter was likely adopted through Steve's parents in England, because Marlene said his parents sympathized with her over Steve's irresponsibility and skirt-chasing.

Medical records revealed that in 1965 Marlene attempted suicide with an overdose of sleeping pills after "a broken relationship." This likely relates to Steve Jeffries.

In the late 60s, Marlene moved to St. Clair Shores near metropolitan Detroit. She joined Promotion, Inc., a commercial auto show that promoted custom and classic automobiles for weekend exhibitions. According to her résumé, Marlene also began to model. Her gleaming smile had been enhanced by creative dentistry.

"I was living off the cuff when I left Michigan," Marlene confessed. In 1968 the auto shows operated out of Oklahoma City, traveling each week to cities such as Omaha, Kansas City and St. Louis. Traveling in a new show car every week became Marlene's circus, her hype. She drove a purple Pontiac from her show circuit to Southern California in 1969. This visit changed everything. Marlene embarked on a new and adventurous life among the jet-set bachelors.

Like her late mother, Marlene was now becoming the stalker rather than the prey.

CHAPTER 14

CALIFORNIA AND TEXAS ALIASES

Marlene was exhilarated by Southern California, its sparkling sandy beaches and fragrant blossoming citrus groves, its striking avenues of palm trees and multi-colored flowers blooming year-round. It was all so gorgeous. The "City of Angels" seemed the perfect place to create a new and vibrant life.

Marlene landed a job as receptionist for a legal firm in Beverly Hills. In 1969 a client named Jim London walked into the office and struck up a conversation. Standing 6'4" and sporting a dapper moustache, London was a swaggering model of dash. At age 35, London was apparently enjoying a career as a small-time construction mogul. He wasted no time getting to know Marlene; the two were soon living together.

"He was even better looking than Clark Gable," Marlene would say years later, commenting on the uncanny resemblance of London to the legendary Hollywood actor. Marlene described London variously as

Cherokee Indian and Canadian, but his family later confirmed he had no Indian blood. London was not Canadian, either; he actually grew up in Peoria, Illinois as Jim Maxwell.

"Jim London" was just one of the many aliases he lived and worked under. As an accomplished con artist, he posed as "Steve McQueen" and "Ralph London." Each time Marlene and her boyfriend moved, their names changed along with their addresses.

London's hair color fluctuated from dark to sandy, and his moustache would appear and disappear. He was variously described as looking like a blue collar worker and as a well-dressed executive. For her part, Marlene was quick to acquire the local provincial dialect wherever she lived. Having lost her German accent in Canada, Marlene turned her talents toward imitating and assimilating the speech and manners of those around her.

When she became pregnant in 1970, Marlene moved to join London in his Irving, Texas apartment. Using the name "Kelin Day," she gave birth to Everett London on January 23, 1971. Birth records show "Ralph London" as the father. The following year, Everett accompanied Marlene to Germany where she masqueraded as a married woman in her native frostbitten hamlet.

Irving adjoins Dallas and Fort Worth, and was Marlene's home from 1970 to 1976. During her odyssey, the Dallas/Fort Worth International Airport opened and the Dallas Cowboys became famous. The construction industry was booming.

Jim London established the Taurus Construction Company, operating out of a warehouse shop and a new office suite. Taurus Construction involved itself in commercial/industrial building, as well as concrete contract work.

Marlene worked as a dental assistant under the name of Kelin London. She drove a new white Thunderbird and dressed as if she were wealthy. Her employer described her as unreliable and mysterious, and perhaps a bit indiscreet in recounting a nude photography session on a bearskin rug to a cluster of co-workers.

Friends in Texas were told that London was her husband, but others knew the two had never married. She kept saying, "I never went by the name London, only Hirsch," but her falsehoods included several aliases in the Dallas area.

It wasn't a smooth relationship with Jim London. He once complained to a relative, "I'd come home covered from head to toe with cement, then be accused of infidelity." According to reliable sources, Jim kept moving around and using different aliases. "He married different women who he didn't always divorce. One lived in Arkansas with a son of London's born a few years before Everett."

Marlene found London to be "an addicted gambler, short-fused, and untrustworthy." They lived a somewhat fragmented life, so she was glad to keep her maiden name or another alias. He would travel from one construction project to another, and disappear from time to time on "gambling binges." She became very lonely during these absences. What she didn't reveal was that she had other lovers at these times.

One day when three-year-old Everett wasn't picked up from the daytime care nursery, the care center phoned the dentist's office. The office manager was shocked that her name had been given to the care center for emergency purposes, as Marlene had never mentioned this to her. The manager was even more shocked when she learned from a friend that Marlene had spent much of the day at a massage parlor after calling in ill.

It was in early spring of 1974 when a member of the dental staff discovered Marlene had applied for a part-time position at a massage parlor. The owner of the dental practice asked the office manager to make out her check, and the next day Marlene was terminated. She "disappeared" and never did repay the balance of a personal loan.

With Irving roaring into the 1970s on the crest of unprecedented growth, the city now had four thriving massage parlors. All four were later raided and shut down for prostitution activities. Marlene's City of Dreams had turned into a nightmare, but her flesh-peddling was just beginning.

*   *   *

Marlene resumed life as Marlene Hirsch upon her return to California in 1976. Jim London became Jim Maxwell upon his return to Peoria.

Jim's relatives had no respect for him. "He suddenly blew into town without having seen his parents or brother and sister in over 20 years," one relative told me. "He would become extremely secretive and was constantly borrowing money and swindling people here in Illinois." Another relative pointed out that, "If Marlene was a liar and con artist like Jim, the match was made in heaven."

Everett, then about ten years old, had blamed his mother for his parents' separations. Rather than live with Marlene in California, Everett defiantly chose to join his father in Illinois. He soon regretted the move. London pulled up stakes and left Peoria, abandoning his new live-in girlfriend and his son. His girlfriend was left with many debts, including payment for the brand new car in which he vanished. She and other creditors, including a local jewelry dealer, tried unsuccessfully to collect sizable unpaid bills.

Everett was described by friends and relatives as a nice lad, but full of anxiety and in need of love and affection. Two families felt sorry for him and wanted him to stay in Peoria with them. He phoned Marlene, however, and was persuaded to fly back and live with his mother in Southern California. After his return, he went to school in the Santa Monica area and joined the U.S. Naval Sea Cadets, a group for 8 to 14 year-olds.

Jim London disappeared and reappeared at odd times, then finally never returned. Marlene claimed he was dead, but admitted she didn't know how or where he died. This was met with skepticism by his brother.

He asked, "Did anyone see the body?" The only certainty was the mysterious disappearance.

Before Everett returned to the Santa Monica area, Marlene moved from place to place six times, always to an attractive, respectable apartment complex. In the late 1970s she lived at the beach in Marina del Rey and fell in love with a married man. Frequently on weekends she and her lover sailed to Catalina Island and San Diego in his 42-foot sloop.

In her words, "With motor and radar we enjoyed sailing at night and spent the daytime in harbor. I learned how to navigate in the galley in heavy seas. Without my motion sickness pills I could have never left port."

In 1979, her lover announced he was returning to his wife. She became so depressed that she took an overdose of sleeping pills and was hospitalized with a resulting seizure. The alienated feelings didn't subside for months while she was seeing a psychotherapist in Los Angeles.

CHAPTER 15

▼

MARRIED MISTRESS

Marlene vowed to never be taken by a man again. Nor did she want to look back—her journal was never resumed after the Texas debacle.

Her self-confidence was gradually regained while working for a plastic surgeon in 1981-82. Since her youth, she had been hyper-aware of her long nose and flat chest. She worried that her appeal and attractiveness had diminished through aging, gravity, and child-bearing.

The plastic surgeon skillfully shortened her nose and inserted breast implants. Now, tiny nipples—the only vestige of her once small breasts— graced the voluptuous bosom she had always desired. Having achieved her goal of external beauty, she concentrated on how to use it. She obtained a Book Club edition of *The Body Language of Sex, Power and Aggression*, and spent hours studying the lessons it provided.

A more stunning hourglass figure may never have roamed Tinsel Town. Marlene's sweet, pert face was often taken for Debbie Reynolds. Marlene began dating two Hollywood celebrities. Chuck Connors, "The

Rifleman," entertained Marlene at his Tehachapi Mountain Ranch. There she enjoyed, among other attractions, his horseback riding skills. The other movie star must remain nameless.

Marlene met more stars while working at an entertainment center near Hollywood. She raved about Clint Eastwood, whom she had "bumped into" a couple of times.

Another prominent celebrity treated her to a summer vacation at a lake in Minnesota. Marlene kept a photographic record of this trip, complete with closeups of her lover seated beside his reddish-brown Irish setter. These prints with negatives were discovered by me in a hidden envelope months after she was evicted from Casa del Vista. Warren Stellar helped make the identification of this famous figure.

In 1982, Marlene secretly filed for bankruptcy. This declaration was coincident with her becoming mistress to Sam (Sammy) Weisbord, the Chief Executive of William Morris, the largest talent agency in Beverly Hills at that time.

"A mistress would never be employed in Sammy's own company," a good friend later said. Marlene worked at "The Agency" for only a short time after Sammy began courting her. Weisbord expeditiously transferred her to a nearby entertainment firm in Century Plaza where she worked as an accountant.

"Sammy started in the mailroom of William Morris Agency, where I was first assigned," said Marlene. "Clint Eastwood was one of our clients," she added proudly, placing him above stars Warren Beatty, Elvis Presley, Sylvester Stallone, and Frank Sinatra. It was obvious she had a crush on Clint.

The legendary mailroom of William Morris has been the subject of several books, because this is where so many top executives in Hollywood began their careers. Among these entertainment luminaries are Michael Ovitz, Barry Diller, and David Geffen. A position in the mailroom may sound like a modest assignment, but staff members sifted through scripts and headshots, and made initial decisions about prospective clients.

Historically, the mailroom position has been a career-launching status symbol.

Sammy was 70 years old when he met Marlene. She said, "He kept me, but not at his place. I cooked for him and accompanied him on trips in the plane he co-owned. He treated me well, and I loved him."

Sammy was wiry and slightly built. His sparkling smile was enhanced by his perennial deep tan and silver hair. Every weekday morning he was up at six for an hour-long workout in the gym. At the Agency he was an efficient dynamo, yet full of captivating charm. Sammy's exuberance surfaced at company functions, where he'd exhort his agents to the biggest year ahead. "The Agency was his life," said a friend.

From his penthouse high above Sunset Boulevard, Sammy could look out at the broad expanse of the blue Pacific and reflect on how far he had come since his employment at his parents' corner store in Brooklyn. He was now at the top of the agency dynasty.

A non-smoker, Sammy learned that he had lung cancer in 1983. It was later diagnosed as terminal. Not until December 1984 did Sammy complete his Last Will and Testament. Marlene had hoped she would be treated the same way as Sammy's mentor had treated his own mistress, leaving her $350,000 and a condo in Palm Springs.

Most of Sammy's estate was left to his temple and to a sister. Nothing to Marlene. Before his death, Marlene had already recognized that she was not to be included in any codicil, so she terminated her services to concentrate on other lovers.

Later, when Marlene was asked by another multi-millionaire to be his mistress, she replied, "I've been there before. No thank you."

*   *   *

It was in the early 1980s that Marlene met U.S. Naval petty officer, D.J. Washington, through a computer dating service, *International Diversions for Singles*. This African-American was about ten years younger than Marlene. She said the two exchanged pictures and became pen pals, but their courtship proved to be much more torrid.

Marlene is believed to have been carrying Washington's baby when she joined him in Hawaii in 1984. His ship, U.S.S. Ranger, was a huge aircraft carrier docked in Honolulu. After meeting at a Waikiki hotel, Marlene received the first of her many Hawaiian leis. The next day, February 22, 1984, the two obtained a Hawaiian wedding license.

After a romantic honeymoon on Maui, D.J. returned to his carrier, whose home-port was San Diego. A tragic fire later occurred in the Indian Ocean during its six-month mission in the Western Pacific, and it was sent to Seattle (Bremerton) for extensive repairs in dry dock. Marlene stayed in Los Angeles to have their baby, hoping it would be light-skinned. It was black, so she made plans to have it adopted in Germany.

The marriage was doomed from the outset, as it had become obvious the marriage was "open" and one of convenience. But with her U.S. residency assured, she was humming along to her tape, "Hey Little Dreamer, you've come a long way."

After Everett was born in Texas in 1971, Marlene wanted to have her tubes tied, but lied that she had a hysterectomy in 1973-74. In truth, the hysterectomy took place after her black baby arrived. Her mood elevated due to the elimination of existing and potential problems and the end of her menstrual periods. The doctor said her sex life would be as good as ever if she maintained the proper hormone levels. With the proper maintenance of these hormones, Marlene actually claimed that her sex drive was measurably increased.

In September 1986, the unconventional mistress filed for a quick divorce, and D.J. acquiesced. No attorneys were used. She had placed the date of separation as August 1985, but in a divorce amendment she changed the date of separation to March 1986. This seven-month difference may have been due to a rekindling of the romantic flame during a Navy shore leave. They reunited near the spot where they first met in

Hawaii. Everett accompanied her, and they spent time at Waikiki beach and Sea Life Park overlooking Makapu Point.

The period between marriage and the original separation was only one and a half years, of which D.J. was away for over a year. Although legal papers were submitted for the divorce, it was not finalized. Records show that the two remain legally married. Thus, Marlene Washington is still in a position to claim D.J.'s pension when he dies.

Occasionally, Marlene would visit D.J. in Pensacola, Florida where he had retired from the Navy. She maintained that D.J. still wanted her back. In 1991 she reported the two might reunite, but after returning from a summer sojourn with D.J., she changed her mind.

"He was no longer alcoholic," she said, "but no longer sexually appealing either. His mind was on computers."

Marlene avoided showing photos of D.J., saying, "He didn't like to have his picture taken." Even Davnet, her best girlfriend in Los Angeles during the period of her marriage, didn't know she was married to an African-American. And Davnet lived directly above Marlene in a two-story condominium complex!

*   *   *

One of Marlene's longest relationships was with Dr. Wallace Weller, a professor emeritus of an illustrious Los Angeles university. She described him as "a distinguished six-footer with white hair and trim build." Indeed, he was also a noted author and a leader in the business world.

When Marlene started to do bookkeeping work for Wallace Weller in the early 1980s, he was still married to Harriet, his first wife. The Wellers were listed in the Blue Book of Los Angeles and belonged to the most exclusive country club in the area. Together, Wallace and Harriet, a real estate broker, owned over 25 properties in Southern California. Of special interest to Marlene were two magnificent retreats, one on the ocean front near Santa Barbara and the other on Lake Arrowhead.

Marlene developed a social as well as business relationship with Wallace. She described her relationship this way:

"I accompany him to brunches, dinners and the theater. He likes to squire me around, especially to the Los Angeles Country Club."

"What type of work do you do for him?" I asked.

"His personal bookkeeping and sometimes errands. Wallace is a real workaholic and it's all business during the day. He's very strait-laced and believes in everything being prim and proper."

"I guess he pays you by the hour?"

"No. $400 cash for each visit. Since there's no record kept of these payments, it's tax free income for me."

"It's a long drive. Do you stay overnight?" I asked.

"Sometimes. But our relationship is strictly platonic."

Marlene had convinced me that Wallace Weller was impotent, and that his terminally-ill wife had wanted Marlene to succeed her in caring for Wallace in their luxurious Santa Barbara estate. Interestingly, Harriet had died in 1986, three years before Marlene concocted her story. And it was Marlene who actually pressed for a live-in relationship with Wallace.

After Harriet's death, Wallace began courting Polly Byers, a pretty widow about twenty years younger. They entered into a confidential marriage in October 1990 and divorced in 1992.

Marlene visited Wallace while Polly was away on trips. In 1991, Polly became aware that Marlene insisted on spending Christmas with him at his Santa Barbara home. Polly knew that Marlene had approached Wallace about moving in with him, and that she had coaxed him into giving her large sums of money.

"Everett is broke," Marlene would complain to Wallace. "If only I had the means to help him get on his feet."

Occasionally, Wallace attempted to disguise phone calls received from Marlene while Polly was there. Polly came to realize how aggressive and determined Marlene was. Her skill at deceiving and manipulating seemed a natural talent, enhanced by past associations with con artists. Her eyes always seemed to be on the prize.

Polly spoke convincingly of Wallace's virility and manly vigor, denying Marlene's story about him. "He's a very strong man for his age, and far from impotent."

CHAPTER 16

▼

DESERT GAMES

The Palm Springs desert of Southern California was even more attractive to Marlene than the coastal area. It had long been called the "Golf Capital of the World" and the "Playground of the Stars." She had flown to Palm Springs on occasion with Sammy, and another time with a boyfriend who was a pilot.

Fred Pyle, a tall and lean 70-year-old golfer, brought Marlene to the desert from Los Angeles in 1986. His new residence in the Palm Desert Resort Country Club became a shelter for Marlene.

Fred helped her find work and rent a condo from his 60-year-old golf partner, a big, jovial Minneapolis businessman who wintered at the resort. Mr. Summers confided, "Fred met Marlene in Marina del Rey in 1986. He generally meets his girlfriends in the pool area of a resort and doesn't choose them very well. One fleeced him for over $5,000 and left a $2,000 phone bill unpaid."

Warren Stellar had trailed Marlene to the home of Fred Pyle after my final meeting with her at Cactus Pete's Restaurant. Before Stellar gave me his reports on Pyle, I had no inkling of his existence.

While Marlene was Summer's tenant, Summer divorced and the two became close. One of his neighbors grinned and winked at my investigator when it was hinted Summer might have been involved with Everett's mother.

Summer told me, "I had no problems with Marlene, but I had to watch Everett like a hawk." At age 15, Everett had "almost burned up my place and caved in my carport roof."

When we spoke, Summer was evasive about his cozy relationship with Marlene, and turned the conversation to her relationship with others:

"Marlene tried to entrap a couple of doctors, but got fired when their wives discovered the affairs."

*   *   *

One doctor's wife was willing to talk about her husband's romantic entanglement:

"Marlene was hired in January 1987 as an administrative assistant and receptionist," she said, "hired not by the doctor, but by the owner of the medical center. Before long, her affair with my husband was full-blown, despite my going back to work in the same clinic.

"Marlene even started leaving nude photos in my mailbox. A nude man in one picture could have been my husband. I was furious and confronted him. I told him that either she had to leave or I'd leave."

"Then you leave," replied her husband, matter-of-factly.

This is just what Marlene wanted.

"Marlene continued to plant nude photos of herself and one was discovered at the front counter by my son," said the doctor's wife.

"That's when I had it out with her. I took Marlene outside the office building and told her off."

"You want me to resign, don't you?" asked Marlene.

"Absolutely! Now."

Marlene finally left the clinic at the end of the year, asking the doctor for a handsome severance package. By then, however, her little blackmail scheme was no longer working and Marlene became vengeful.

"I started receiving threatening phone calls," continued the doctor's wife. "And even my private investigator couldn't put an end to that. She's a pervert and very sick. She must enjoy sending nude photos to wives, or to anyone she thinks she might be able to blackmail or eliminate as a competitor."

At the same time Marlene was seeing the doctor, she was pulling similar tricks on a suave and charismatic oil dealer. Using the patient list from the doctor's office, she had scoped out this senior gentleman who became attracted to her. Before he knew it, Marlene had mailed a pornographic photo to his steady girlfriend.

"Marlene tried to solicit money from me," the oil dealer recalled. "She besieged me with cagey phone calls and letters. Then one day at the clinic, she showed me my chart and told me the doctor said I had less than a year to live. She knew I had no family and no beneficiaries, and she was lying about my diagnosis. When she began bringing me unprescribed medicine for my heart, I became suspicious and didn't want anything more to do with her."

Marlene rented successive condos in the Palm Desert area with Everett at her side. When she vacated them, three landlords reported broken leases and monies owed. Her boasts of being a "neatnik" proved false, as she and her son left behind an assortment of trash.

In April 1988, Marlene served as receptionist in a new dental office where she dated clients and was described by the good-looking dentist as a "horny bitch." When she was forced to leave, she joined the dentist across the street.

Marlene became front-office manager for the distinguished Dr. William Randolph. In this position, she scheduled and received all of his patients, a veritable Blue Book of esteemed names.

Marlene was immediately attracted to Dr. Randolph. He was congenial and handsome, a soft-spoken man in his late fifties. His hobby happened to be horseback riding. Highly regarded in dentistry, he was admired in the community and reputed to be a faithful husband with seven children. Despite her flirtations, Marlene was unable to convince him to stray.

*   *   *

For all her conquests, Marlene had not been a beneficiary of an estate. This changed after Marlene moved in with 62-year-old Max, a rough-hewn contractor and investor whom Marlene had dated the decade before in Los Angeles. Max was going through a messy divorce from his fifth wife. He was also a patient of Dr. Randolph, which is how he and Marlene reconnected. Soon thereafter, she moved into his impressive home.

Max's macho character and megabucks appealed to Marlene despite his being a heavy drinker. They attended polo events together, played tennis, and went horseback riding, yet the two quarreled a lot.

Marlene and Max separated in October 1989 after only five months together. When Max's divorce became final in December, he joined the singles club at his church and started dating other women.

"I left because of his unrealistic demands," she claimed. "He was stubborn. Things were always done his way."

A year later Max had a serious stroke that left him paralyzed on the left side and affected his speech. Marlene said he had no desire to go on as an invalid. A proud man, he couldn't imagine life without his gift for gab.

Since his latest girlfriend was no longer in the picture, Marlene moved into his home to care for him and administer medication. "HOME-CARE" was inscribed on a business card she distributed to eligible men, but in truth she had no training as a nurse. Max needed 24-hour skilled nursing services, and reportedly, he resisted these.

Marlene stated that she and a chiropractor friend removed his liquor and guns, but forgot about the Japanese World War II rifle kept in a prominent cabinet. In the early morning hours of Sunday, March 25, 1990, Max allegedly took the rifle and shot himself.

Marlene had left early Saturday evening. She knew his ornamental gun was in the cabinet but said she hadn't realized it was loaded.

"I hadn't known what deep feelings I had for Max until he committed suicide. Why didn't he take his pills? Why did he choose to die? Why didn't I stay there all the time?"

Two days before his death, she helped him scrawl a one-page holographic will that included her in the estate. Her chiropractor friend, who acted as executor of the estate, was left $5,000 by the crude will and Marlene $2,000. The remainder was willed to his church.

Would Max have drafted a will that alienated his children? They believed their father had been coerced into signing the will and, of course, contested it. Eventually they were awarded half the church shares; however, the small cash awards to Marlene and her friend remained intact. Marlene and the executor, who were referred to as "strangers" on the court documents contesting the will, were undoubtedly aware of his many outstanding debts. By the time the estate was distributed, it had shrunk to a pittance.

Numerous questions about the suicide were raised by Marlene's insistence on writing the will only two days before his death and by later investigative reports. If Max thought his liquor supply and gun collection were removed from the house, how did he know the ornamental rifle was still in the cabinet and that it was still loaded? With his partial paralysis, would he have had the strength to put the long gun to his head and pull the trigger? How depressed did Marlene leave him when she left for the night?

Most importantly, was he under sedation when he awkwardly scribbled his will, and what was the toxicology of his body when he died? Warren Stellar wondered whether his remains should be exhumed and analyzed for poisonous doses. As might be expected, it was learned his body had been cremated.

*   *   *

Mel Rautman was a good-looking 72-year-old German who met Marlene after he placed a singles ad in 1989. Rautman lived in an elegant condominium in PGA West. The two played tennis and frequently dined at home, with Mel doing the cooking.

Marlene had told me what a good cook Mel was, emphasizing that theirs was a strictly platonic relationship. She said she helped translate official letters he received from Germany.

Mel put the relationship in a slightly different perspective. "We liked each other and got along well. We spent a couple of hours together two or three times a week. She never stayed overnight, but we had a good sexual relationship and traveled together."

Mel had mentioned an interest in real estate investments. Before he knew it, Marlene was showing him a new residential development not far from the polo grounds. She had already chosen her favorite two-story model.

"This one would be your best investment, and I'll pay a rent that will almost cover your monthly payments." The two signed a three-year lease before the home was ready for occupancy early in 1990.

Marlene submitted lists to Mel for additions to both the interior and exterior, including some creative landscaping. He paid for these, but when she tried to coax him into construction of a lap pool and a solarium, he drew the line.

Upon completion, Everett and a roommate moved into the spacious dwelling along with Marlene. Then 19 years old, Everett stood six feet tall and was thin as a rail. He was poorly groomed but, like his mother, sexually active.

Mel became upset at Everett behavior. "He was a lazy, sleazy character. I discovered Everett had inscribed a bold swastika in the wet concrete of my new patio. That did it! I was steamed."

Shortly after Mel refused to give Marlene a loan, she broke the three-year lease and stripped Mel's place. She left it in such disarray that Mel sued Marlene and won *two* court judgments. Mel never collected, however, because Marlene declared Chapter 7 bankruptcy.

Marlene was so angry at Mel for cutting her off, then suing her, that she didn't stop at declaring bankruptcy. She counter-sued and attempted unsuccessfully to get the case on television.

Even the judge couldn't believe his eyes when the charges were read in civil court: "BREACH OF PROMISE OF LANDLORD TO PAY FOR SEXUAL ENCOUNTERS"!!

CHAPTER 17

▼

THE WILD POLO SCENE

The polo grounds were a powerful magnet for Marlene. Located just minutes from my desert home, the exclusive Polo Center offered world-class equestrian competition, with celebrity participants who ranged from Prince Charles to Sylvester Stallone. Marlene dreamt of owning her own horse, but most of all she had a white knight fantasy, pursued relentlessly during her equestrian years.

In youth, she had cherished the German tradition of classic horsemanship, beginning with trips to Hamburg where she would watch performances of the eye-catching Lipizzaner and Andalusian stallions.

At the Polo Center she was smitten with the breathtakingly beautiful thoroughbreds and the equestrian Disneyland of nearly one square mile. Dressed in her tasteful Saks Fifth Avenue high fashion ensembles, she appeared poised and comfortable while watching events from a fieldside table. She definitely knew how to make the most of warm sunshine, a patch of green grass, and admiring eyes upon her.

Polo is a flashy sport and very rough to play. Those who have become addicted to the game call it the greatest of sports. They say the best place to learn to play is at the Polo Center.

A business associate of mine described her recent first-ever polo match:

"It took a lot of persuasion from my team before I risked my life on the field. Polo is such a unique combination of horses and players. It's not like driving a car, because the polo pony has a mind of his own. To control this 1,200 pound thoroughbred, you not only have to be focused, but extremely strong. You use every muscle in your body and wind up perspiring and spent. It's dangerous out there, because you know you could be hit by a ball or a mallet. Hitting the ball while traveling 35 miles per hour takes a lot of practice, believe me. And you feel so courageous for having competed in this fast and furious game."

Marlene enjoyed the color and excitement of polo, but was not herself a participant. She preferred the off-field tranquility where she could parade her horse in front of players and club members. Nothing flamboyant. The "trim ex-model," a phrase she liked to use in her singles ads, took pride in wearing quality riding outfits and mixing with riders in a coquettish manner.

Marlene may have loved the horses, but her passion was for the horsemen: the 200-plus male polo players, trainers, and owners. The elite lifestyle of some captured her attention, but she had a penchant for the tall, rugged cowboy type.

One polo veteran said she would not date male players:

"They are such scumbags, hosebags, and they'd boff anybody and everybody. While I was playing polo I was considered one of the guys, and they'd talk in front of me about their conquests. One day they'd be sleeping with one girl, and the next day another. They're changing partners all the time, and some are having affairs with wives of other players."

She described her male polo group as chauvinistic and machismo: "They are so macho that even in this day of AIDS they refuse to wear condoms."

Most of the members of the polo clubs were well-heeled attorneys, doc-tors, or successful businessmen. As a result, many of the girls who rode on the grounds pranced in front of their marks and played up to them. Party time was anytime. A quick tack room boff was not uncommon.

Marlene quickly learned the inner workings and the hierarchies of the club system, even working for a short time at one of the polo clubs. She was considered a second-rate horsewoman, a very private person, and quite feminine. Fellow riders said, "Marlene would walk her horse around and rarely canter or gallop. She was far from being a skilled rider."

Nevertheless, Marlene wrote a former friend about her love of riding:

"When I took up riding four years ago, someone said I would get tired of it in a year or so. So far there has been no sign of that. The more I ride, the more I find real enjoyment in it. I really do enjoy the great outdoors here. But the summers are just too darn hot. I ride my horse when I can con my riding partner into getting out of bed early, or after 7:00 P.M. when it cools off."

Although Marlene wrote of owning her own horse, she was actually just a guest in the saddle. This is one reason why the name of her horse seemed to change often.

Marlene saw the movie *City Slickers* several times, and became attracted to the idea of trail riding. She saved newspaper and magazine articles on the subject. What motivated her most was the opportunity to charm an experienced horseman into acting as her trail guide in the undisturbed back country. She began to bike daily after reading that bicycling was the best way to get into condition for a long ride. For prospective trail com-panions, Marlene would provide vivid descriptions of romantic retreats that dotted the Western wilderness.

She seemed to concentrate on one trainer at a time, often bartering for services. One example was a 40-year-old polo trainer whom she first flirted with in 1991 while wearing a low-cut top and tight-fitting jeans. He confided to a close friend how she had invited him to her nearby condo "to share a kiss or two."

Marlene said she cleaned his tack room and shoveled horse manure in exchange for use of a horse and the cost of its maintenance. She told someone else that the bartering involved the preparation of the trainer's taxes. Actually, her "horse trading" carried a sexual connotation.

Whether a rider was young or old, a factor that would register was his physical prowess. One young trainer she pursued was known among the women to be "humongous." His principal female companion was frequently at his home when Marlene would call. He would act annoyed, at least in front of his girlfriend. This trainer was known to be lazy and a real loser, but Marlene would arouse him in one way or another for an early morning ride. His girlfriend remembers his balking one day after Marlene had paid a visit. "I'm sore right now. Looks like my job is to keep you women happy," the trainer said.

When Marlene was asked, "How's your love life?" she'd often use a favorite expression, "Not too shabby." A horseman told one of his girlfriends, "You wouldn't be happy if you knew who else I'm sleeping with now."

"I knew it had to be Marlene," she said, remembering the sinking feeling. The liaison was later corroborated.

Marlene refrained from inviting most of her senior live-in companions to the polo grounds, but accepted their treating her to rides at distant ranches. The polo grounds would remain her private retreat.

She was a strategist, and knew how to employ the right approach to make a man feel unique and special. Nearly all of her non-polo suitors were hoodwinked into thinking they were the sole object of affection. And Marlene always acted in such an innocent manner.

Marlene was asked by one female polo player how she could maintain so many lovers. She answered disarmingly, "Guess it's just my nature." Had a member of the polo set not already been nicknamed "Skippy," the girls might have pinned that name on Marlene, because she skipped from one guy to the next.

"I take more showers during the day than anybody I know," Marlene would say. "I take one when I get up in the morning, when I get back from riding, after I go swimming, before and after sex, and before I go to bed at night."

Marlene may not have been a champion rider, but she certainly had sport in her blood. Even if she never competed on the polo field, some wondered if she were trying for the world's boffing championship.

CHAPTER 18

NEW MYSTERY PATTERNS

Almost immediately after being evicted from Casa del Vista, Marlene secretly contacted my ex-wife, Lucille.

"Brad is a drug addict!" Marlene said. "I'm frightened of him! I had to move out because of his wild mood swings."

To prove her point, she mailed Lucille a copy of a Temporary Restraining Order against me. When we met for the last time on April 23, 1993 at Cactus Pete's, Marlene told me that this Order was never intended to be permanent. "It served my purpose," she said. Marlene had wanted to deflect suspicion about the poisoning.

She knew that Lucille harbored a grudge against me after losing two divorce judgments, and now learned that Lucille planned to sue me for $100,000 "blood money." She offered to assist Lucille in the suit. The reaction of Lucille's grown son was reported as, "This is just the break we need to sue Brad."

Lucille passed the word to some of my friends, "Brad has divorced me. I've lost everything." In reality, she had unloaded two of her properties on me by breaking her written and verbal agreements to be responsible for these and other personal debts. I had to repossess the properties after our second divorce, first her luxurious RV, then her residence in a desert resort 30 miles from me. Her creditors were able to bypass our written agreement and nail me, because I had co-signed her loans after our first divorce in order that she could qualify for credit. The mortgage guarantees were a favor to Lucille that backfired.

Before I repossessed Lucille's desert residence, I received a tip from a friend that I should pay an inspection visit. It was late April, just days after I had met Marlene at Cactus Pete's. My confidential source told me Lucille's home had flooded after she had abandoned it. He hinted that the main irrigation valve had been turned on to full strength and allowed to run overnight.

Who was responsible for this small disaster? Two weeks later, I received a midnight phone call from a motel in the desert. It was Lucille's plaintive voice.

"I know I'm breaking the Restraining Order between us, Brad. Could we meet tonight and inspect the residence while it's dark?"

When I met her at the site, we found the locks had been changed. Unable to enter, we retreated to a nearby 24-hour restaurant where we talked until 5:00 A.M. Ostensibly, she was offering help in dealing with the water damage; in reality, she wanted to make certain that I knew she had nothing to do with the mysterious flooding.

It was in the restaurant that Lucille first learned about my being poisoned. She was shocked. It took her some time to understand she had been recruited into a double-game by Marlene.

"Brad, you ought to have that woman prosecuted," she said. Later Lucille learned from Warren Stellar the complications of such a case. The investigation would take months and a court trial could be long and arduous. And who wouldn't be afraid of criminal defense lawyers who can, in good conscience, vigorously defend the accused even though they know they are guilty. Stellar flatly stated, "All investigators know people who are guilty of murder or attempted murder, but are walking around free." Scary!

It would take only one misguided juror to create reasonable doubt and prevent my winning the case. While we knew Marlene was guilty, Stellar and I had observed how often the scales of justice are weighed inaccurately and unfairly.

*   *   *

Lucille extended her stay in the desert for several days in order to help me in the collection of more information about Marlene, and prepare a joint civil suit against the resort for the water damage.

"After Marlene first contacted me, she invited me to her workplace," said Lucille. "There, she talked in a non-stop monotone for most of six hours."

Lucille was astonished Marlene could talk about traumatic events so glibly and without emotion. Marlene volunteered to testify against me if Lucille brought suit for "blood money," my price for her vengeance.

"I sent Marlene a long list of additional questions to answer," Lucille said. "I promised that I'd pay her expenses to return to the desert in case she decided to move away with her current flame, someone from the resort where she was working. He had talked of taking Marlene to one of his office locations in Chicago or Denver."

Lucille secured Marlene's permission to tape-record a six-hour monologue, which included an account of the Saturday I was poisoned. "*We* went out to the polo grounds," Marlene began. Then she quickly changed this to, "*I* went out to the polo grounds alone, because that was my sanctuary, and I never showed him the barn that I occupied." She failed to mention that she had invited me out to the lake that morning for photographs.

Marlene told Lucille, "When Brad removed his garage door-opener from my bicycle pouch, he overlooked his decals."

At the time, I had no idea these windshield stickers had been intercepted in the mail by Marlene three months before. I had peeled from her windshield the only one I knew to be in her possession. It was unknown to me that new stickers for 1993 had been issued in December. When I removed the garage door-opener, it was pitch dark in the wee hours. I remember touching some papers at the bottom of Marlene's bicycle pouch, but I was in a hurry to prepare her eviction notice.

A month after her eviction, a letter from Marlene was mysteriously delivered to my private compound.

"It was Marlene herself who had made illegal entry to PGA West," Lucille confided to me. "She used one of your entrance stickers and continues to boast about her entry."

A security officer confirmed that a lady of Marlene's description had come to the guardhouse that afternoon. Inside the guardhouse, one could easily view pictures on the wall of Marlene with her hair up and in a topknot. This time, as never before, Marlene entered with her hair free-flowing to shoulder length.

Security management took action and issued a warning letter to her, "You are currently recognized as the one who deposited a letter [at Mr. Dunaway's residence]…this matter has already been reported to the police." The case number was cited, and the suspicious circumstances of her entry after her previous eviction were pointed out. Naturally, Marlene never honored Security's request to return the gate decals, and I certainly wasn't prepared to prosecute the poisoning case.

Lucille sketched a diagram of a secret entry to Casa del Vista that she herself had once planned to use. "Marlene will probably take advantage of this route along the golf course fairway. She's out to get you," Lucille insisted. "She never loved you and she admitted rifling through your personal effects while you were in the hospital." This became obvious when I checked my files.

"Marlene was hopping mad at your cancelling a trip last fall to Dallas," Lucille confided. I remembered then how vexed Marlene had appeared, because she had planned to visit a former "best girlfriend" from the 1970's. An investigator later discovered that in actuality the woman hadn't heard from Marlene in years and seemed to have no special interest in seeing her again. I wondered what male liaison(s) in Dallas/ Irving she had in mind while I was busy with my golf tournaments. And how many times had this happened on previous trips? Marlene covered her tracks well.

Marlene was doing her best to alienate Lucille against me. Spawning suspicion and harassment had always been part of her game. Lucille had contacted the Secret Service about a pornographic photo she received in the mail the day she returned from Florida in 1992. Thinking it was from Marlene, she visited with the same agent I had contacted and shared the following with me:

"The agent said the Secret Service thought Marlene Washington might be an accessory in the Luis Rodriguez case. They told me that a sting operation had been devised the summer of 1991 in which Marlene was encouraged to maintain contact with Luis on weekends. She apparently didn't follow through."

I now realized that the Secret Service agent deliberately lied to me when he said Marlene was not considered a suspect in Luis's scams. This, I'm sure, was to prevent me from telling Marlene that she was known to be involved.

*　　　　　*　　　　　*

Marlene was still in love with Luis Rodriguez. Lucille had recorded the following:

"I was deeply in love with this man. All I had to do was touch his hand and shivers would run up my spine…and he didn't seem real anxious to get me in bed right away. He moved in with me the fall of 1990. Everything was wonderful for several months and then I became suspicious. He was really a con man—I really loved him—and I'm not over it yet."

I didn't suspect how much Marlene had aided and abetted Luis, partly because of her relentless criticism of him and partly because of her exposure of his crimes. After her eviction I discovered she had removed many of her spiteful letters about Luis from my files. In addition, the letters prepared jointly by us regarding Luis had never been received by the Secret Service and my Congressman's office. Most likely Marlene never mailed them. I reflected on how much Marlene and Luis were truly mirror images of each other.

I was beginning to understand why Marlene had seem displeased when I continued to pursue the Luis Rodriguez case just before the poisoning. The new Secret Service agent had promised me he would give the case priority, and this had alarmed Marlene. After the poisoning, I had gone to the Secret Service office and shown the agent the evidence that Marlene would no longer make a credible witness against Luis.

"My predecessor should have completed this case," the agent said. He disclosed they now knew where Luis was living. Unfortunately, this was a piece of information I passed on to Marlene at our meeting at Cactus Pete's before I knew she might be assisting the con artist.

Marlene phoned me after I had spoken to the agent. She demanded, "Don't contact the Secret Service anymore. They don't want to hear from you." I thought she was lying, but it was actually a forceful message to "get lost."

Warren Stellar visited the Secret Service four months later on the pretense he was looking for Luis. The Secret Service once again had lost track of him. They asked Stellar to let them know if Luis was found.

Stellar solved the mystery of Luis's whereabouts after locating a traffic citation for him in January 1994. Luis was living as Bert Tilman in Long Beach, California.

It had become apparent to Stellar that Luis was being used as a cover man for the Secret Service, probably as a street snitch to identify drug dealers or other con artists. As a bounty hunter, he would be paid for hunting and rooting out bigger game.

"The Secret Service isn't interested in convicting Luis or Marlene," Stellar told me. "Reporting to them on Luis is as futile as turning him in to the Water Department. Your original private investigator should have never recommended that you take the case to the Secret Service."

It is sad that a revered federal agency would stoop to such shameful practices.

           *   *   *

Lucille revealed all of the letters that had been exchanged with Marlene *prior* to the poisoning. Nevertheless, she did not find out that Marlene lived with me until *after* the poisoning. All of the correspondence prior to the poisoning was written during September 1992, the month the divorce was originally scheduled to become final.

Marlene had shown me the first letter she received from Lucille, a letter addressed to her private post office box. However, she kept denying any further contact with Lucille throughout the last six months that she lived with me. I now knew each woman had sent two letters to the other.

Lucille corresponded first, "Marlene, I strongly suggest, if you haven't done so since your relationship with Brad ended (or has it?)—that you get tested for the HIV virus…why am I bothering? 'Because I'm mad as hell and I'm not going to take it anymore!'" She asked Marlene to collaborate with her on a book about justice for women, a subject Marlene said appealed to her. Her implications about my having AIDS were considered libelous by my attorney, as I did not (and do not) have the HIV virus.

Marlene answered by mail that her HIV tests were negative and "I am not interested in supplying data for a book…hate is a most useless emotion. I hope you put it to rest."

Marlene had planned to send Lucille a third letter after the divorce. It was found on my computer after her eviction. She accused Lucille of playing a con game, taking me to the cleaners, and previously scheming a suicide attempt in my company offices in order to remain with me. She wrote:

"Had [Brad] been any other man, he would have told you: Hang on a second while I go to the rest room; then he would have called 9-1-1 and [have you taken] away in a straitjacket…" For once, Marlene had hit the nail on the head.

Marlene's deep-rooted hostility to wives and ex-wives of her lovers was chronically demonstrated by vicious and retaliatory letters. She contrived stories, mixing reality with fantasy, and acted as if she was the wronged person, rather than the destructive predator.

Lucille told me that Marlene thought I was a cheapskate, citing as an example my budgeting only $5,000 to redecorate the master bedroom. I had to smile as I remembered how Marlene pretended to be thrifty. She showed no understanding of the limitations of retirement income, and spent much faster than my nest-egg permitted.

In one phone call to me after her eviction, Marlene poked fun at the Christmas ring she had once proudly displayed. I played the message for Lucille, who said Marlene now referred to the ring as "a piece of crap" compared to a $6,000 diamond from another beau.

Interestingly, Marlene never had her Christmas gift from me sized to fit. It was a lame excuse for not wearing it at work. And yet in the last photo of us together, taken at a special event the month before the poisoning, she is cuddled next to me and proudly displayed her engagement ring.

Was the poison attempt a way to get rid of me and make room for somebody else in our private Casa del Vista? Lucille later confirmed that this was Marlene's intent. I now wonder how many secret affairs she had at my place while I was away on trips.

Perhaps Marlene should have been named "Lorelei," after Germany's blonde siren of the Rhine River, whose beauty and haunting songs lured sailors to shipwreck and ruin.

CHAPTER 19

▼

CONSPIRACY PLOT

Warren Stellar was not only a superb investigator, he was also a mediation expert in divorce cases. During Lucille's visit to the desert, she learned of Stellar's skillful investigation of the poisoning episode, and then reviewed his credentials. She agreed to have him mediate settlement of her debts that I had inherited after our second divorce.

The three of us met at a desert restaurant where the grievances of both parties were aired. After the initial discussion, Stellar asked me to sit at a distant table so he could examine the situation privately with Lucille. An hour and a half later, Stellar came over to my table and confided:

"Lucille realizes what deep feelings she still has for you, Brad. She wonders if there's any chance you two could get back together. It might help her emotional state if you would let her know."

I returned to the mediation table and explained there was no chance of reuniting. This was an obvious disappointment to Lucille. The session ended without a firm resolution, although we both agreed to a mediation period lasting 60 days, and longer if necessary.

"I really regret having made this trip out to the desert," Lucille told me the next day. "What an error I made in seeing you."

"But Lucille, your heroic acts have actually saved the day," I reassured her. "You've provided valuable information, especially about Marlene. Certainly you did the right thing. Please continue to help the investigation, and mail me a copy of the transcript of your tapes and Marlene's answers to your questions." Hesitantly, Lucille agreed.

We renewed our verbal pact to exchange information about Marlene. Lucille was naturally more interested in what Marlene said about me, and I more interested in what was said about Marlene. I did not expect Lucille to spy for me, only that she pass along new information as it came to light. Upon her departure from the desert, it was comforting to know that we were united against "Ms. Poison."

Lucille surprised me by phoning earlier than expected. She was agitated and wailing after receiving overnight Stellar's written report.

"Oh what a mistake I've made. You two set me up!" she accused Warren Stellar and me. "My children would have a fit if they knew I spent time with you on my desert trip."

Lucille was upset with Stellar's report. In my mind, Warren Stellar had done the best job possible to represent both sides fairly, but she considered him my employee and felt that he produced an account that was embarrassing to her.

The part of Stellar's report that most concerned her was this paragraph:

"L.D. [Lucille] said that this meeting has revealed that she is still in love with B.D. and she will always consider herself 'Mrs. Lucille Dunaway.' She said that she wants him to tell her face to face that he no longer loves her. She said that until he does, she will continue to have 'emotional problems.' B.D. was told of the request. He told her he no longer had any interest in her but would like to remain friends. She felt that was what she needed to hear."

Could Lucille show this report to her children or other relatives? Probably not, because they might then become reluctant to help in a future lawsuit against me. It was obvious that Lucille's children had absorbed their mother's views on the divorce, and more important, had been kept in the dark by Lucille on key aspects of our relationship.

Despite her apparent misgivings, Lucille continued communication with Warren Stellar. Her principal objective was to determine how much money she might obtain in damages. When asked point blank by Stellar, "What are your damages and what do you want?" she replied, "I would be revealing my case if I told you." Repeatedly, she told him her plans were to file a family case as well as a civil suit, yet she was never clear on what issues were in dispute. She intimated that I had coerced her into signing agreements. I began to sense Stellar's frustration.

A second mediation session was held in early July. This time Lucille refused to have Warren Stellar participate. At the meeting, I told her that I wanted to make my mediation proposal as flexible as possible, given that Lucille might not always be able to work full-time. I suggested she consider starting a business at home, setting her own hours. Lucille declared she was working on a book, but had a rightful suit against me for the blood money—because I divorced her. Needless to say, no further progress was made on negotiating Lucille's debts to me.

Faced with the termination of our mediation period, Lucille requested an additional 15 days beyond the original 60 days in order to change attorneys. Anticipating her failure to mediate the settlement, I filed legal papers and was automatically awarded an Entry of Default, in the amount of $29,000. Before I could collect this money, however, Lucille filed for Chapter 7 bankruptcy. Her petition showed few assets and many debts, the largest being the monies owed to me.

By phone, the Bankruptcy Trustee who was hearing the case befriended me. He explained why I shouldn't squander money on a lawyer, and told me how useless it would be to appear in court in light of the unfair bankruptcy system that favored debtors like Lucille.

*   *   *

Marlene had been a major subject of discussion at our second media-tion session. Lucille spoke at length about Marlene's new beau. She told me that Marlene's lover from her resort workplace had been replaced.

At that session I asked, "Where is the tape transcript and Marlene's answers to your long list of questions?"

"That's cold coffee, Brad," she replied. "I am not going to give it to you."

Cold coffee. The expression was so familiar. It is a peculiar German idiom that roughly translates to "let bygones be bygones." Since Marlene frequently used the phrase, it became immediately obvious the two women were again in close communication.

"Do you remember Mrs. Taratino, my old next door neighbor?" Lucille inquired. "She noticed that you placed an ad in the paper seeking a part-time secretary-bookkeeper."

"What would an 83-year-old woman be doing looking through the employment section?" I asked suspiciously.

Lucille backed down, and admitted she had actually received a copy of the ad from Marlene. As our discussions continued, it became apparent how much Lucille's subterfuges were beginning to resemble Marlene's. Lucille had offered Marlene confidential information about me, and Marlene had done her best to throw wrenches into the works. Thanks to Marlene, Lucille was now convinced I had "hidden assets" which might be tapped through legal sleight-of-hand.

Communication broke down after the second mediation session. "As long as we're in a deadlock," Lucille informed me, "I will not be disclosing information about Marlene."

Extortion! Without my giving her blood money, my ex-wife would now be cooperating with Marlene.

I doubted Lucille's stability. "If I had known Marlene was living with you, I would have brought my gun and blown you both away," she had confided. Although she had wanted to buy a gun while we were married, I balked because I did not want one in the house. But I knew Lucille had purchased a gun after our second divorce while living alone. Knowing the power of Lucille's wrath, I had not wanted her to know Marlene had moved in with me.

Lucille began telling friends in 1993 that I never loved her and that all I did was use her. I could not believe that Lucille, much more intelligent than Marlene, could be brainwashed by a woman known to have lied. She realized Marlene was infected by greed, lust, anger and foolishness.

Yet that summer as the stakes mounted, Lucille arrived at a crossroads. Should she continue to join forces with Marlene, or side with me? She opted for a third path. She would provide information to both Marlene and me, then join Marlene in the joint lawsuit against me.

An informer told me that conspiratorial phone calls between the two continued into the fall of 1993. Lucille shared with Marlene confidential intelligence I had received from Stellar concerning Marlene's romantic activities.

Lucille promised me that she would never divulge my writing a book about the poisoning episode. She also promised not to release confidential information about Everett, and was supposed to keep Warren Stellar's investigations a secret. In the end, she spilled everything and betrayed me on all counts.

With the alliance launched between Marlene and Lucille, it was Brad Dunaway pitted against the two, with Everett prowling in the background. How weird!

Marlene phoned Warren Stellar in late July, representing herself as "Cindy Thompson."

"What will a background investigation of my boyfriend cost?" she asked.

She scheduled a meeting with Stellar the next day at Cactus Pete's Restaurant. She said she was 5'5", with long brown hair, and would be wearing a white dress. "Cindy" added that she would bring pictures, implying that they were of her boyfriend.

The next morning, "Cindy Thompson" phoned Stellar at 7:45 A.M., just after arriving at her job. She said she would have to cancel the lunch meeting, but would phone and arrange to meet the next day. Stellar recorded her call because he thought it was Marlene. I later positively identified her voice.

Lucille said later that after Marlene was to meet Warren Stellar for lunch, Everett phoned his mother at work.

"Mom, I was followed today by two people in two cars." As a result, Marlene never phoned Stellar again to arrange another appointment. Everett and his girlfriend immediately moved out of Marlene's residence. He became associated with dopers outside of the Coachella Valley, and despite filing for bankruptcy, established a "shell" business while still sharing his mother's bank and investment accounts. Through bankruptcy, many of his mother's debts were written off under Everett's name. Once his bankruptcy was discharged in 1995, he opened a weapons order business out of his new residence in Palm Springs.

Several informants reported news of Marlene and Lucille's impending lawsuit against me. The suit would claim that I had never loved Lucille and that I had manipulated her affections. Marlene planned to testify on Lucille's behalf and share the rewards of a large settlement. Both women furtively schemed to go to the media, and even to appear on television. The conspiracy alarmed me, not because I feared a lawsuit, but because I was concerned that my safety was now in jeopardy. To what lengths would Marlene go?

*   *   *

Much later, I learned about Lucille's last lunch with Marlene in late 1993. Marlene brought an array of photographs to show Lucille what handsome men she had dated. Lucille was unimpressed, and told Marlene how much she deplored her lifestyle. Indeed, Lucille's lifestyle, as well as that of most women, was sharply in contrast to Marlene's.

It was the end of a friendship of convenience. United against me, the two women formed an effective team. Although they had been outspoken enemies, they had joined to seek reprisal, but while woe and misery make good companions, they do not make for an enduring bond.

The lawsuit was never filed.

Unfortunately, Lucille had not invested her settlement monies wisely and nearly wound up wearing the proverbial barrel. Meanwhile, Marlene was still impeccably dressed, and riding in a Rolls or Jag with yet another Sugar Daddy.

CHAPTER 20

▼

THE SCHEMING APHRODITE

"How much did Marlene take *you* for?" asked an earlier Sugar Daddy when I introduced myself. Marlene admitted to Lucille, "My philosophy is to get as much as I can from everybody in my life." A friend recalled Marlene boasted she'd have a million dollars in 20 years.

Marlene's closest friend, Davnet, didn't trust her. She confided to me how Marlene had interfered in her relationship with the most important man of her life, a well-known priest of a large local church. Davnet was in love with him, but her strict Catholic upbringing would not allow her to become intimate. When she told Marlene her feelings, Marlene scoffed at her and predicted, "It won't be long until you're in bed together."

One evening, Marlene baby-sat while Davnet and the priest went out together. On their return, Marlene stayed in the apartment and chatted with the priest, who had brought frozen yogurt for her. Davnet could not help but notice that Marlene was taking his generous and charismatic manner as flirtation.

Marlene joyously told me about meeting the priest at Davnet's home. She gushed, "Oh, he's so much fun!" I could tell how enamored she was, not realizing then that she anticipated seeing him at the Saint Patrick's Potluck hosted by Davnet and scheduled for the same Saturday evening I was hospitalized.

Marlene did her best to build a relationship with the priest. The following week, she was able to obtain two tickets to a concert Davnet and her son were planning to attend. She arranged to have the priest join the group and, by controlling the tickets, made sure that her seat would be next to his. It was a big disappointment when he canceled at the last moment.

Marlene had given me the impression she was attending the concert with a girlfriend, so when she phoned that her girlfriend couldn't attend, I was elated to join her. And yet Marlene acted strangely through the show. In retrospect, this was because her planned flirtation with the priest had gone awry.

Weeks after the poisoning, the church received an anonymous phone call from a woman who informed them that the priest was having a love affair with Davnet and was violating his oath of clerical celibacy. The priest and Davnet believed that Marlene made the call, hoping to disgrace the pair. This was not the first time Marlene indulged in *Schadenfreude*, joy in another's misfortunes.

Despite this apparent betrayal, Davnet did not want to give up her friendship with Marlene. When Davnet told her about the mysterious phone call to the church, the schemer refused to discuss the subject of the priest. He was a dead issue. "That's cold coffee, Davnet," Marlene said.

Marlene's devious schemes included one revealed on my computer. It involved Countess Binaldi, a wealthy American who had once been married to an Italian aristocrat. The Countess was known to be fond of Dr. Randolph. Marlene tried to help her lure and trap the married dentist. She wrote Countess Binaldi:

"My boyfriend grew up in your home town (in Illinois) and he would love to take you to lunch...As for me, I would like to talk to you concerning my favorite boss, Dr. Randolph..."

At the close of the luncheon, which was held in Countess Binaldi's elegant home, I was dismissed so that Marlene could explain how Dr. Randolph needed a wealthy widow in order to retire. Several days later, a hometown friend asked me Dr. Randolph's age. When told the dentist was about 20 years younger than the Countess, my friend joked about it. "He may not be young enough. Her Italian count was much younger, and so were other husbands."

The amount of Marlene's financial gain in this business transaction was not divulged, and now I wonder if Marlene was really trying to entrap Dr. Randolph for herself.

While living with me, Marlene completed a four-month weekly modeling class for newspaper, radio and television commercials. She graduated with a diploma, a new résumé, and an outstanding composite photo for booking purposes. Although her slim-trim type was then popular, her only casting call was unsuccessful. Undaunted, Marlene switched talent agencies and hoped for the best.

After the poisoning, I visited Marlene's modeling instructor, a handsome 55-year old bachelor. As an agent, he had placed many top models and came highly recommended. "Marlene fancied herself as another Marlene Dietrich," he recalled. "She fluttered her eyelashes and really tried to come on to me."

Stellar told me that wherever Marlene went she seemed to be overdressed, a silver hook to professional men and potentates. She was especially attracted to plastic surgeons who offered fringe benefits. One surgeon referred to her as a "plastic surgery freak," because she had at least six breast procedures, three nose jobs, and two facelifts.

A married neighbor later spoke about an incident that occurred when he was working in the side yard next to her rental house.

"One summer morning Marlene emerged from her garage in an old warm-up outfit," he said. "Upon seeing me, she quickly went back inside her house. Minutes later she came out wearing a low-cut, tight-fitting T-shirt without a bra. Her breasts were amply displayed and her nipples clearly outlined."

After months of taciturn greetings to the neighbor, this was the first morning he was engaged in pleasant conversation.

Curtis Turner had been one of Marlene's chief targets before Luis used Curtis for credit card fraud. Marlene said that Curtis asked her to become his mistress in 1989. Then in 1990, Curtis took advantage of his wife's extended summer absence and became an overnight guest in Marlene's rental home. His distinctive Nevada car collection had been noted by neighbors during these trysts. In light of the Rolls Royce and Mercedes-Benz cars parked in her driveway, they suspected Marlene was a lady of the night.

Marlene and Curtis Turner were observed coming and going in riding togs. Turner had paid for a horse, for additional plastic surgery, and had showered her with gifts. This would have been mere pocket change for him.

Following Marlene's termination from Dr. Randolph, Curtis Turner testified against Marlene at her Workers Compensation Hearing. At this proceeding, Marlene brandished written testimony of a second offer to become Turner's mistress, hoping to embarrass Turner in front of his wife. It was little wonder Curtis Turner never returned my phone calls. At the time, he probably found himself cornered and subject to her blackmail.

Marlene may have longed for a permanent relationship, but her history of unsuccessful and short-term love relationships made this unlikely. When affairs faded, usually within a few months, Marlene would be off and running again. She didn't like to discuss the reasons for broken relationships, and usually offered the terse explanation, "He expected too much of me."

A virtuoso at her art, Marlene kept her compulsive tendencies hidden from even her closest acquaintances. Her few friends knew only the smiles and the laughter, not the multiple liaisons. Like a busy attorney, she attempted to juggle four or five clients at once. Her decision to go to work at a distant desert resort was at least partly motivated by a desire to expand her clientele and establish a reasonable alibi for her frequent absences.

I was never aware of being sexually manipulated, as Marlene's lovemaking was always passionate, and she invariably seemed caring and unselfish. She never withheld sex as a punishment, threatened to have sex with others, or avoided sex with "a headache." She loved making love, and was honest about using it as an outlet for frustrations. Had she been asked about the frequency of sex with me, she'd be inclined to offer a wry response. "Hardly ever. Maybe four or five times a week."

Most adults have sexual fantasies, although Marlene claimed to have none. So I was taken by surprise in December 1992 when she left a type-written fantasy on the kitchen table:

THIS IS A DREAM

Date: 11:00 A.M., 1992
PLACE: The highway between Las Vegas and Barstow

"You are behind the wheel of a late model sedan, and I am sitting in the passenger seat, reading you a short story that you took along for the trip to Vegas. I look up and spot a small side road coming up. I suggest you pull over and we get out and stretch our legs. After we get out and take in the typical scene of cactus and a few old abandoned homes, I get into the back seat and motion for you to follow. You have a puzzled look on your face,…"

Marlene followed this with an account of heated sexual passion. Afterwards, she wrote,

"…you reach for me, and again we linger in a kiss. There are no words spoken, but I can tell from your touch you are happy, and I am."

Marlene never brought up "The Dream" after leaving it on the kitchen counter, and I never mentioned it to her although it clearly reflected her thinking. Much later, I discovered that she also gave a copy of "The Dream" to one of her trainers at the polo grounds. It was strange behavior, of course, for a woman engaged to be married. How many other lovers received "The Dream"?

Marlene told me in 1990, "Every healthy relationship has therapeutic effects." I didn't realize then how many relationships she had, nor how "healthy" she must be.

*   *   *

Marlene's addiction to lying may have been as strong as her addiction to sex. She frequently perjured herself: for example, she declared under oath that she had never filed for bankruptcy before 1992. In front of a judge, she lied that I had coerced her into signing legal documents by threatening to "misshape" her face.

Marlene admitted forging my name to a bogus letter she shared with Lucille the summer after the poisoning. She had tried to make it look like I promised to marry her while still married to Lucille.

Aliases were part of Marlene's con artistry. More than 15 had been uncovered at the close of the investigation, plus six or seven used by Everett. Frequently, when relating a story about a friend, she would use a false name; as often happens to liars, she would accidentally use a different name when retelling the story. After her eviction, I came to learn that whenever Marlene would speak a name—horse, mate, friend or casual acquaintance—one could only be certain of the correct sex.

It was not surprising that Davnet found Marlene frequently distorting the truth. Davnet said, "Marlene actually believes you're paying me to give you information." This accusation disturbed her a great deal, as she feared her young son might be in danger. She knew Marlene was dishonest and untrustworthy. And yet it was her anxiety about Marlene's possible recriminations that kept Davnet speaking to her, but only as a cautious friend.

Deviousness seemed to have no boundaries for Marlene, even where her fondness for animals was concerned. In late 1992 she told me her son received a puppy as a Christmas gift from his girlfriend. I suggested that she make certain that Everett keep his pup at home and not at Casa del Vista, knowing how irresponsible he was, and how attached Marlene and I might become to it.

Marlene was well aware that I loved dogs. The statue of Candy on display in my courtyard was mute testimony to my affection for the dog I had owned for many years. Candy, an Irish Setter-Sheltie mix, was the last of many dogs which had lived with me in my lifetime.

Several days after Christmas, Marlene showed me a photo of "Everett's present from his girlfriend." She exclaimed, "Isn't that a cute puppy? It's a German Shepherd-Labrador mix."

She began hinting anew how much she would like to have one. "Isn't this a cute puppy?" It was a phrase I heard often, as magazine and newspaper photos were put in front of me.

Marlene started calling from work during the day, pleading with me to get her a puppy. The phone requests soon changed in tone from coaxing to threatening, "If you don't get me one, I'll have Wallace Weller get one for me." I reiterated that a dog might interfere with our summer travel plans, and even more importantly, with our own relationship before it was firmly established.

The day after the poisoning, I entered ahead of Marlene through the garage door, looked out to the large courtyard, and couldn't believe my eyes: A PUPPY! Already upset at Marlene, and suspicious that Everett was or had been in the house, I immediately escorted the five-month-old dog to the courtyard gate and waited to see if it would stay or leave. The puppy scampered out.

Marlene watched me do this. Barely holding her anger, she offered an explanation. "I saw you do that. The puppy was a stray that wandered into the courtyard when the paramedics opened the gate on Saturday. How could you be so cruel as to release a stray dog?" Speaking carefully and with an air of assurance, she added, "I would have phoned tomorrow and placed the dog with an animal shelter if no one claimed it."

Marlene had forgotten she had shown me the picture of Everett's present. She insisted Everett hadn't been there, and the animal had no connection with him.

The next morning, wanting to make certain the puppy had been rescued, I called the front gate and learned that one of the security guards had taken it home. After Marlene had left for work, I sifted through the garbage and found remnants of pages from my diary chronicling Marlene's many requests for a puppy.

Weeks after Marlene was evicted, I had brunch with a married couple close to me. The wife remembered a conversation she'd had with Marlene three months prior: "She told me that the puppy, a German Shepherd-Labrador mix, was a gift to her from her son. She didn't want you to know that."

Although I hadn't really doubted it, this was the first time I could be certain that the "stray" had belonged to Everett and Marlene. The big mystery of the small dog in the courtyard had been solved!

Marlene could be just as deceptive in her singles ads. She discovered a cost-free way of meeting men, since the burden of payment was put on those who dialed the numbers to hear the scripted voice messages. Marlene continued to place ads almost every week, so that new conquests could be found in the desert.

Her advertisements generally sought a "tall, trim, fit male, 40 to 70 years...who's not afraid to share life's *pleasure* with this special 40+ lady." She had become a "HUG THERAPIST," a curvaceous ex-model who was a "one-man woman." Marlene professed to being European with "Old World standards," and deplored "game-playing." She offered "TENDER, LOVING CARE in large doses" and "fun times." Her expressed interest in "small airplanes and fast cars" was obviously aimed at the jet set.

I wondered how Marlene kept her many fabricated stories straight, and I reflected that my batting average was zero when she made her pitches to me. However, it would take a group of forensic psychologists and psychiatrists to offer full insight into her cunning and conning nature.

CHAPTER 21

▼

MARLENE, A PSYCHOPATH?

The fascinating, chilling world of psychopaths gradually came into focus as I wrote this book. However, it wasn't until the story was almost complete that the dangers smoldering inside this type of personality became crystal clear. Once I understood the profile of a psychopathic personality, the resemblance to Marlene was striking.

Dr. Robert Hare, the expert on psychopaths, has developed a *Psychopathy Checklist*, a clinical tool for professional use by forensic psychologists and psychiatrists. He has summarized the key symptoms of psychopathy as follows:

- conning/manipulative
- promiscuous sexual behavior
- short-term relationships (many)
- parasitic lifestyle
- glibness/superficial charm
- lack of remorse or guilt

- pathological lying
- callous/lack of empathy
- impulsivity
- irresponsibility
- criminal versatility
- antisocial behavior

From *Without Conscience* by Robert B. Hare, Guilford Press, 1999. See also *No Conscience, No Remorse* by Robert B. Hare, Maclean Hunter (Canada), 1996.

Dr. Hare points out that psychopaths are not "psychos." They are rational individuals, aware of what they are doing and able to exercise free will in doing it. In contrast, when a psychotic individual attempts murder, he or she is generally declared insane. A psychopath who is found guilty of the same crime is sent to prison as a sane person.

Dr. Jack Levin, a criminologist, points out that the majority of psychopaths are not killers or people who *need to kill*. However, they can kill without remorse if killing becomes expedient.

According to Dr. Levin, it is a frightening combination when a psychopath is also a sex addict, working to satisfy personal needs with numerous voluntary partners. There is less guilt to inhibit a person like Marlene.

Psychopaths differ from pathological liars and manipulators by the ease and extent with which they lie, and by the callousness of their deceptive plots. During our last months together, Marlene probably realized she had created a monster, trying to please me without truly loving me. How long could she deal with this?

Two months before the poisoning episode, Marlene became intrigued by the 1992 movie, *Basic Instinct*. She rented a copy of the videotape and viewed it without me. Days later, she typed a revised cohabitation agreement for my consideration. It contained the new stipulation, "in case Brad expires before I do."

Marlene purchased a videocassette of *Basic Instinct*, which arrived in the mail shortly after her eviction. Curious to see what prompted her to buy it, I watched the film for the first time. The movie portrays not only promiscuity and psychopathic behavior, but hateful obsessions and utter disrespect for human life. Marlene's ultimate plan contained similar elements, including manipulative games and methods of casting suspicion on others for a homicidal act. The movie demonstrates how a psychopath might strive, like Marlene, to minimize her own personal jeopardy while protecting a loved one, like Luis, from authorities without losing the opportunity to reunite with him.

Marlene was also intrigued by the 1987 movie, *Black Widow*, in which Theresa Russell portrays a serial murderess who becomes rich by poisoning her husbands. In the film, autopsies do not reveal the poisonings, because only toxicology screens are run and not quantitative tests. As a result, large overdoses of the poisoning drug go undetected.

Movies not only distorted Marlene's reality, they provided her with potential plots and scenarios. She would use whatever macabre plan best matched her target.

Professional psychologists agreed that Marlene's characteristics were those of a psychopath. Psychopaths accuse *others* of being too nosy. "Don't ask questions; you're always asking too many," Marlene would say. It was a frequent rejoinder, although I rarely inquired about her personal activities outside the home.

A psychologist told me, "Marlene will go to any lengths to cover her tracks. This is a woman capable of poisoning good people in order to escape the pain of revealment."

In evaluations by two psychology clinics in 1992, certain of Marlene's test results were off the charts owing to "exaggeration of symptoms." At the time, she was thought to be exaggerating in order to achieve a better score; in retrospect, the tests may have hinted of an underlying psychopathology. Her brain pattern on an electrical recorder would be most revealing.

Although the examining psychologists may not have known it, they scored Marlene high on the *Psychopathy Checklist*. Test results showed "narcissistic traits, with denial and repression as a defense mechanism." Marlene was shown to have both personality and behavior disorders with histrionic, hypochondriac, antisocial and suicidal tendencies. It was noted there were two Marlenes: the persona projected, and the person she really was.

Marlene told me she had tears in her eyes at the Workers Compensation hearings, and also at her therapy sessions. This came as a surprise because I had never seen Marlene teary. No matter how sad or emotional the situation, she wasn't outwardly affected. Feelings of that sort were well-shielded, if they were present at all.

Her riveting, emotionless stare proved to be a prelude to exercising power and control. I had mistaken the look as one of detached interest, or even the beginning of empathic caring.

As her false pretenses and alibis came to light, I was struck with the realization that the only response I could count on from Marlene was an unexpected one. There was no question she was an impulsive personality, and I always had been aware of this impulsiveness. But her many hidden schemes and subterfuges—her blueprints for blackmail—indicated a deeper and far more disturbing pattern.

To Marlene, an apology or act of contrition was a sign of weakness. It was not enough to simply deny the accusations against her. A much higher level of control was sought. To remain strong was to be absolutely unrepentant. Marlene was compelled to delude others into thinking *she* was the victim and *I* the evil aggressor.

"You never loved me," she had said when she departed Casa del Vista—a complete inversion of the true situation.

"He wanted me as his sex slave," she told others. This was yet another outlandish reversal of roles.

"He wanted to extract a $150,000 settlement from me—he was after my money," one more characteristic example of Marlene's transfer of guilt.

These assertions were completely foreign to those who knew me, yet it was surprising that some people initially believed her when she told them her concocted version of events. "I was never evicted—Brad begged me to stay," she would say. "Brad is a crazy maniac."

Even Davnet could not believe Marlene's complaint, "Brad is a Halcion addict and I had to leave him. It's a beautiful home, but I can't stand it there."

Nanette, who had divorced a con artist, could not swallow Marlene's letter to her. "Brad is a Jekyll and Hyde and I couldn't stand him."

With the passage of time, as was Marlene's custom, these stories changed and were never consistent.

I learned that psychopaths do not have the capacity to feel guilt or remorse for doing wrong to others, since they lack a conscience. Marlene had no shame. In jest, I had once suggested that her numerous nightmares might be related to a bad conscience. She pondered this a bit, but didn't seem to accept it. At the time I didn't realize she had no conscience.

"She looks like someone who has everything going for her—like the nice girl next door," a friend pointed out. Indeed, when people met Marlene, they couldn't conceive how this affable woman might kill another human being. How many of her acquaintances would believe this possible? Very few, even when they were made aware of her criminal past.

My friends and family members detected no odor of evil when they were with Marlene. Her outward shows of affection served to divert suspicion. Although I was much closer and often puzzled by her actions and reactions, it was only after the poisoning that I began to discern the terrifying pattern.

Several individuals close to me asked how I could be deceived for so long, implying that they would not have been as trusting. Dr. Hare offered an answer:

"Some people are simply too trusting and gullible for their own good—ready targets for any smooth talker who comes along. But what about the rest of us?...The sad fact is that we are all vulnerable. Few people are such sophisticated and perceptive judges of human nature that they cannot be taken in by the machinations of a skilled and determined psychopath. Even those who study them are not immune; as I've indicated...my students and I are sometimes conned, even when aware that we're dealing with a probable psychopath."

I didn't weigh an evil intent any more than I would contemplate being pushed into the path of a speeding car by a friend. Yet for Marlene, the poisoning was just like squashing another bug.

What are the chances of Marlene being healed by therapy? Unfortunately, this dream won't be realized. One authority spoke of psychopathic behavior as "not just a disease, but the ultimate disease."

"The transformation of Marlene into a person with a good heart is as mythical as kissing a frog and turning it into a princess," I was told.

How common are psychopaths? They appear to be everywhere among us. Recent data suggest three to four million in North America alone. Sociobiologists believe the number is increasing.

My hospitalization proved to be a small price for my survival. Nevertheless, I never dreamed that there was no real safeguard from her predation. Many more skeletons may be hidden in Marlene's past. But could any of them offer a clue to what lengths Marlene would go to exact revenge?

CHAPTER 22

▼

IF TOMORROW COMES

If Tomorrow Comes is the name of a Sidney Sheldon book published in 1985. I remember this significant title, because the book was loaned to me by Davnet Duggan shortly after she heard about the poisoning.

Davnet and I only knew each other socially through Marlene. After Marlene's eviction, I was asked to give Davnet some of Marlene's belongings left in my garage. Davnet invited me into her condominium for coffee and to see her 12-year-old son. While there, I had the opportunity to ask about her Saint Patrick's Day party which I had missed because of my hospitalization. Our discussion led to my sharing the poisoning episode.

Marlene claimed to be very close with Davnet, but I discovered that she never told her "best friend" that she and I were engaged to be married. Concealment was one trait in Marlene's lifelong pattern of deceit.

Davnet then told me about a suspected insurance scam, in which Marlene claimed to have broken her foot at Davnet's condo in order to benefit from the homeowner's insurance policy. Without doubt, this was not the first time Marlene had made a false claim.

Davnet and I agreed to keep these disclosures confidential for the time being. Later, over the phone, she confided that what I told her was extremely heavy. She said she was having a hard time accepting the poisoning after being Marlene's friend since the 1980s when Marlene lived in the apartment below her. Marlene came to Davnet's assistance after being physically abused by her husband. When Marlene heard the fights overhead, she would call the police. Subsequently, she supported Davnet in court against her now-divorced husband.

I knew Davnet sympathized with my plight, but aware of her background with Marlene, I suggested a delay in our talking together again. Marlene would undoubtedly continue her attempts to demean me in front of Davnet, so I didn't want to put her in an uncomfortable position.

I understood how livid Marlene would become if she knew I was talking to any of her friends. To her, image was everything. The slightest invasion of her private domain was considered a threat. Later, when Marlene did discover that my informers were on good terms with some of her confidants, she became extremely upset.

"Marlene is obsessed with harming you, and is out to get you!" one told me.

Another put it even more bluntly. "Marlene tried to get a guy to attack you."

How would Marlene accomplish this? Although my number one priority in life was to move on from the traumatic events surrounding our relationship, the tracking of Ms. Poison consumed much of my time.

*   *   *

When I learned that Marlene had received $20,000 from the cosmetic surgeon's insurance company, I became increasingly concerned. What would she do with this additional money in her hands? She was marshalling her emotional resources into revenge. The settlement gave me yet another reason for bolstering security at my home.

Despite my Restraining Order, Marlene kept sending letters, first to my attorney and then to me. She would usually pretend they were from someone else. From the style of typing, the capitalization of all nouns (as in German), the typical reversing of my initials, and certain idiomatic phrases, the origin of the letters was clear. The return addresses often turned out to be non-existent.

"Marlene has a habit of shooting herself in the foot every now and then," Warren Stellar told me. "She doesn't realize some of her actions are as transparent as glassware. You'll hear from her whenever she thinks she can sabotage you."

The hoaxes continued from 1993 through 1996. Marlene went to absurd lengths, ordering subscriptions in my name to at least 20 magazines. She also sent over two dozen "gifts" through the mail. All subscriptions and gifts were charged to me, of course.

Davnet's reaction was, "She thought you'd really be annoyed."

My local postmaster quickly diagnosed the mail fraud and suggested I file a complaint. However, I felt that pursuing this matter aggressively would be like playing with a rattlesnake. Marlene would only turn around and bite me again in another spot.

Identification of the many new men in Marlene's life proved a formidable task for my investigative team. Warren Stellar's male friends had attempted to answer her voice ad, but Marlene never responded. Stellar thought it was because she was waiting for a candidate from PGA West. His theory had ominous implications and seemed to hold water.

Marlene's answering machine messages at her home number changed periodically to suit Marlene's romantic moods and aspirations. They varied from, "This is the residence of Marlene and Everett…" to very sensuous messages. Her accents varied from French to British to German. I remembered Marlene's affinity for the English, which she considered the "most cultured" and aristocratic of accents. A French accent, by contrast, was "the most sexy."

One night an informer's tires were slashed and I received menacing calls, accompanied by diabolical laughter, probably by Everett. My terrified informant believed the slashing was done by Everett and Marlene's polo trainer. The victim was so distraught that she moved from the desert immediately after her car was repaired.

A few days before the vandalism, my informant had rented a guest house that the polo trainer had planned to rent. My friend later learned that Marlene and the polo player resented the move and blamed the new tenant *and* me. The couple had planned to use the guest house as a secret rendezvous spot. Their last hideaway had already been discovered by his other lovers and by my investigator.

"Jackass, jackass," whispered Marlene. It was just one of many angry messages left on my answering machine.

"You'll pay," she threatened in another. Was this zany zealot a time bomb ready to explode?

Davnet had promised to phone whenever she became concerned about my safety. Months later she alerted me that Marlene was seeing a plastic surgeon in PGA West. This worried both of us.

After I notified the security guards at PGA West, Marlene was caught entering the gate by displaying one of the two gate decals she had stolen from me. Upon being confronted by the guard, she said the plastic surgeon was her husband. A series of additional lies followed, most of them documented in written reports supplied by security personnel.

That February I took a beautiful young lady to the Saint Valentine's Day party at PGA West, having learned that the plastic surgeon was a notorious womanizer. It was easier meeting him than we had expected. He became attracted to my companion and introduced himself to us. Over the course of our conversation, it became obvious that he was a bit tipsy. Our visit lent itself to my warning him that one of his lady-friends was a

Black Widow. Upon learning I meant Marlene, he thanked me warmly and returned to his table.

Davnet later told me that he phoned Marlene the same night. Two days later I received a threatening message from a male voice, later identified as the doctor.

"If you'd refrain from harassing her, I'd really appreciate it—or else you may be looking for a plastic surgeon."

Despite this surgeon's reputation of "re-building his women and then building a relationship with them," it was surprising he would leave an anonymous message that would so obviously identify and implicate him. He would *not* be the last man Marlene conned into phoning me.

I started to receive an increasing number of menacing phone messages and numerous hang-ups. What was brewing? There was a sense of mystery. When I found the light bulbs in the courtyard unlighted and deliberately unscrewed, it seemed as if Marlene was on the brink of another fanatical plot.

Late one afternoon, soon afterwards, a small piece of cement was thrown at my master bedroom window. Panic-stricken, my housekeeper ran from the room. Marlene's evil intentions were becoming abundantly clear.

I began to worry more when I read that contract-killer fees had fallen sharply on the current market, owing to the spread of contracts among drug addicts and gang members. Could Marlene's malicious mischief, combined with Everett's contacts in the drug world, create marketable mayhem?

Since I was living alone, there was no one else to call an ambulance in case of an evil misadventure, or as Marlene would call it, "an accident." After all, my pen and voice had almost been stilled before, and I wanted to make doubly sure there would be a tomorrow.

It was time to purchase a portable cellular phone. I carried it in my pocket wherever I went. It also could be used as a backup in case my home telephone lines were cut or became inoperable. I immediately programmed the phone numbers for my most important contacts, so that any could be reached at the touch of a button.

The first number programmed? You guessed it: 9-1-1, just where this story began.

CHAPTER 23

▼

LOVE TRIUMPHS

I had no inkling that the year 1994 was to be filled with my brightest tomorrows. It all began when I decided to travel to Europe in the spring with my oldest son. The trip would include a few days in Germany where Marlene's stories of her youth might be validated. As I explored various avenues to locate a suitable German interpreter, I remembered Ramona.

While in her Palm Desert shop the previous summer, Ramona's German accent supplied the tip that she might make a good translator. She had been kind enough to translate a note in German left by Marlene in my master bedroom upon her eviction. The essence of the note:

"Suicide—would be the easy way out now. There is no life left at present. The sun has gone to places unknown for me. Why bother to go on?"

It also spoke to my becoming *"ganz geändert,"* totally changed; *"viel Sauerkeiten,"* very bitter.

From other notations on the page, I concluded it was probably written before the poisoning, and certainly before Marlene's eviction. She had planted the note deliberately. Davnet suggested that she was playing upon my sympathy.

By coincidence, it was Marlene who had introduced me to Ramona's business in 1992. Now, returning to the store a year and a half later, I asked Ramona if she knew anyone in the Hamburg area of Germany who could assist me with genealogical and other research.

Ramona spoke briefly about governmental information sources and then kiddingly added, "If you'd buy me a ticket to Germany I'd go with you."

The more I pondered it afterwards, the more sense it made. I'd not only have an interpreter, but a German guide through the country. Also, Ramona's wish to see her mother and brother would be fulfilled.

The following day I returned to Ramona's shop to discuss the feasibility of this European trip. It was also important to determine her marital status, as well as whether Ramona personally knew Marlene. Upon learning Ramona was single, a widow, and outside of Marlene's circle, I felt encouraged to ask if she could get away for at least ten days.

"Yes," she said, although she made no commitment, and said she would be too busy the next three days to discuss it further.

Coincidentally, just after I queried her, Ramona checked her store records and discovered Marlene had been fitted that very same day. However, she didn't recall ever meeting Marlene.

We finally met for dinner to discuss the trip in a business-like manner. One dinner followed another, as we both began checking the other's background.

It took four dinners before she finally said, "You're on." I completed travel arrangements with my agent the next day. Meanwhile, my son was off on his own European tour from San Diego.

Ramona told me of a dream she had the night before I came to her shop. The message was clear: she would encounter someone special coming into her workplace, a man worthy of her consideration. This motivated her to respond favorably when I asked for travel assistance.

Naturally, Ramona was concerned about my having become engaged to someone like Marlene. I had shown her my preliminary manuscript, but she only had time to read one or two chapters. She read the rest of the manuscript on the plane trip to Europe and became even more apprehensive. What was this fellow really like?

Upon arriving late at the hotel in Hamburg, we were greeted at the registration counter with bad news: "I'm sorry, we do not have the two rooms your travel agent requested." Ramona frowned, but hesitatingly agreed to share a room with me. During our stay she gradually relaxed and was able to rest more comfortably. Our business relationship blossomed into a cozy friendship, filled with mutual respect and a promising vision of the future.

I hadn't realized Hamburg was such a nocturnal city. Merchants stay open late into the night, especially on the Reeperbahn, a famous nightclub strip that we visited. The German music and camaraderie relaxed us from our intensive probing of records and people during the day. We danced to the German polkas and enjoyed the Liederkranz into the wee hours.

Each day was like a fortune cookie which we opened to find a new and joyous message. By the end of the journey, Ramona was pleased to introduce me to her relatives in south Germany as her good friend. When we returned to Palm Springs, we agreed it had been the most magnificent and exhilarating ten days we'd ever spent.

Love came upon us unexpectedly, with the fervor and intensity of a spring thunderstorm. We kept rubbing our eyes in disbelief that we had been drawn together so quickly, and that what was happening was real. Once we started holding hands we didn't let go.

Ramona was fifty years old when we met, the only daughter in a traditional German family. After completing the equivalent of an A.A. degree, she had met an American soldier who was stationed near her hometown. Ramona didn't accept his first proposal of marriage, so he re-enlisted for an additional year to win her hand. The two married in Germany.

Ramona's husband was soon transferred to Fort Huachuca in Arizona, and although Ramona had never visited the United States before, she soon found herself immersed in American culture and the mother of four children. After her husband left the service, the California desert was home for two decades before her husband died suddenly of a heart attack at age 46. I was relieved to learn Ramona was no longer grieving for her late husband.

By running two shops, Ramona put all four children through school. This meant long hours of dedication as a tailor, designer, teacher and store manager. Ramona's work ethic was impeccable, and I was soon aware of how well-liked and respected she was in the community. It was not surprising to find out that she had won "outstanding service" awards in local media opinion polls.

From the start, it was apparent she was a far different woman from Marlene. Ramona was genuinely pleasant, with a quiet aura of peace and tranquility. She was sensitive in mind and spirit, and soft and gentle with everyone. We had the same feelings, interests and outlook.

I felt absolutely safe when I was with her. This was one gutsy and intelligent woman, who knew no prevaricating or rationalizing. Ramona was beautiful, and her movements were graceful and sensual. After our European adventure, our minds and hearts were one. The music had begun, and both of us were ready to dance once again.

*   *   *

When ex-wife Lucille offered to visit the desert again in the spring of 1994, I was presented with a delicate situation. "As a good Christian," she said, "I want to assist you in your flood damage lawsuit." Lucille added that she was seeking peace with the world as her health problems were escalating. Her assistance proved invaluable, because she was the custodian of records and information regarding the damage to her former residence.

Ramona bet me that Lucille was out here to win my affections, and was naturally apprehensive of my ex-wife's visit. I promised that Lucille would never set foot in Casa del Vista again, and she never did.

Upon arrival, Lucille lost no time in asking whether I was dating anyone special.

"Yes," I said, "I currently have a serious relationship."

Lucille didn't press me for details, but upon learning Ramona's name and place of business, she conducted her own clandestine surveillance of the shop, no doubt hoping to get a look at the new woman in my life.

Lucille showed me a letter she received at Easter from Marlene. She also showed me her prompt reply, requesting no further correspondence from Marlene. Lucille wrote that Marlene had distorted the truth so much she would never trust her again. Privately, Lucille admitted to me some of the mistakes she had made, such as believing Marlene's lie that I had affairs during the nine month period of our *Living Together Contract*.

Lucille again told me of "almost going off the deep end" two summers before, and how she would have pulled the trigger if she had known that Marlene and I were living together. It was at that time she had felt partly the woman scorned and partly the woman in dire straits. I breathed a sigh of relief that Lucille was out of my life.

Lucille had saved a newspaper article for me about another Black Widow who was convicted of plotting two murders. The woman had been dubbed a "green widow" because she spent almost all of her million dollar inheritance on fancy cars, trips and wardrobe.

Never one to be denied, Marlene haughtily responded to Lucille's Easter letter. She prefaced her remarks with sarcasm. "Thank you for your kind note," she wrote.

Marlene then smeared me with references to my being "wild and crazy." She said her friend, the plastic surgeon, believed I suffered from mental retardation. Yes, she was still sneaking through one of my resort's private gates under a fictitious name, and yes, she bragged that she was still seeing the well-known doctor.

In March 1994, Marlene filed suit against me for defamation of character. This stemmed from my telling the doctor she was a Black Widow. She attempted to gain support in the courtroom, but her chief witnesses, the plastic surgeon and Davnet, refused to appear.

Subpoenas were sent by Marlene to Lucille and Warren Stellar, my chief investigator. Both arrived in court but were not called to the witness stand. The judge ruled in my favor, denying all of Marlene's allegations. Legal authorities later told me the judge had decided not to listen to her nonsense. She had no recourse for appeal.

In the hallway after court, Marlene and her attorney approached Warren Stellar and chastised him for not submitting his subpoenaed records. Stellar told them he did not have the documents to submit, but had been ready to testify as a witness. He added that his testimony would be about tracking Luis and his accomplice, Marlene. Stellar further stated that he had checked on Marlene's prostitution activities and would be glad to discuss them. Marlene and her attorney were dumbstruck.

Tenacious as ever, Marlene sprang back into action and sued me again for defamation of character, this time in Small Claims Court for $5,000. Marlene was bitter and boiling. "My numerous health problems have been greatly aggravated by Mr. Dunaway," she told others. "He is a wolf in sheep's clothing, a con artist and a misfit."

Lucille surprised me by making another appearance in court on my behalf. This time she did testify, along with the deputy sheriff whom I had contacted the day I left the hospital. Marlene stormed out of court after the proceedings, but not before she and Lucille had a heated exchange:

"You're a liar, Lucille!"

"I'm not a Black Widow," responded Lucille.

Several other witnesses present agreed that Marlene was a very disturbed individual. Each time in court she committed perjury. How relieved I was when the judge again ruled in my favor and the case was put behind me.

Ramona attended both court cases and was astonished and appalled at what she heard from Marlene and Lucille. "How similar these two appear to be," she commented. I think she wondered a bit about me, too. How could I have had relationships with those two women?

Marlene wrote a series of malicious letters to Lucille on June 29, 1994, the same day she had stormed out of court. When they were returned unopened, she mailed them again, this time using an alias and a fictitious return address. Marlene wrote, "I just hope you don't end up like Nicole Simpson." Would her harassment never cease?

The case for flood damage was heard days later, and Lucille was again ready to leave the desert. We met for lunch and she reflected on the success of her visits.

"Everything has worked out," she said, "except for one thing." She put her hand on mine on the table and smiled. I knew what she meant, but it was too late. We both recognized that I was in love with Ramona, who won my somewhat naive bet on Lucille's motives.

*   *   *

That same year, I received another harassing message from Marlene less than 15 minutes after I passed her on the road while driving in the opposite direction. Attempting to disguise her voice with a thick German accent, Marlene propositioned me. It was a blatantly obscene message, similar to "THE DREAM" that she had once left in my kitchen.

"This woman is sick," friends told me.

Was this call an ill-conceived attempt to entice me to break the mutual Restraining Order? She seemed accustomed to breaking the law, and was even bold enough to send me handwritten letters. They were full of venom and disdain, the antithesis of her love letters. She frequently included leaflets on schizophrenia and mental disease.

Throughout the year, Marlene and Everett bombarded me with hang-up calls, some of which were confirmed by my investigative team. Because of privacy laws in California, we weren't always successful in tracing their origin, but one day in October we hit pay dirt! Within minutes after a hang-up call, my investigator was able to give me the number of the caller. Curious as to who it might be, I waited a few hours, then dialed the number. "Dr. Weiskopf's office, may I help you?" I thanked the receptionist upon learning that Dr. Weiskopf was a dentist.

I didn't have to wonder why a dental office would call me and then hang up. Only a few minutes passed before I received another phone call, which I recorded on my answering machine. This time it was Marlene's voice.

"Oh, what are you spying on me for? Don't you have something better to do? I understand you're getting married again. My condolences to the poor lady. Quit calling wherever I happen to be. I'm not interested in listening to your stupid, ridiculous voice."

Did she not realize that I had traced her earlier hang-up call? It was obvious Marlene had a new job, and was again targeting an eligible dentist. Her search for a dental position had taken over a year, because the word was out among most dentists about her employment record. Six months after obtaining work from Dr. Weiskopf, Marlene was spending her free time looking for another position.

Soon afterwards, a male voice left the following message on my answering machine.

"I think you ought to do yourself a R-E-A-L favor and leave Marlene alone. Okay? I'm not gonna tell ya twice. I just won't tell ya twice. Be careful."

Warren Stellar traced the threat to Nick Celani, the man who housed Marlene after her eviction.

Always on the alert, I tried to avoid Marlene as one would a large sinkhole. It wasn't easy, because she had moved closer to Casa del Vista and frequented some of the same dining spots. Once, when I arrived at a nearby restaurant to meet Ramona and a group of friends, I found Marlene's car parked outside. I quickly steered our friends to another eatery down the street. Later, I learned that she had dined that evening with Fred Pyle, the man who had brought Marlene to the desert and financed her sports car.

*   *   *

Ramona and I were married in August 1994 on a magnificent day, replete with beautiful sunrise and sunset. Afterwards, we sat at a reception table and were toasted: "To many fun-filled mörgens," friends laughed. From our honeymoon hideaway, we could watch remnants of the sunset and see the moon rise. What an enchanting day.

Everyone has their faults, but I was still looking for Ramona's. Lack of caring was certainly not among them. She was as enchanted by the marriage as I was. A time of song, laughter and gaiety reigns at Casa del Vista.

*   *   *

Marlene continued to lurk in the shadows. Christmas Day 1994 found her composing and rehearsing a long message she would leave on my answering machine, and that I would hear days later on returning from vacation.

"You'll get yours one of these days, and it won't be me doing it. It'll be your darling wife, who's already got other plans for you, and who has another lover on the side!"

Ramona and friends burst out laughing when I played this passage. Marlene obviously did not know Ramona. However, it was sad to reflect that Marlene had nothing better to do on Christmas than intrude upon our holiday in such a cruel and insensitive manner.

"I have an inside track that you don't even know about, and if you did, you'd be ever so-o-o upset," Marlene stated contemptuously. Her inside track was actually through one of my own informants, operating as a double agent, a woman who was having an affair with Marlene's polo beau but who was herself unaware of Marlene's intimacy with her boyfriend. My spy had left her lover early Christmas morning, mentioning in passing that I had gotten married. Six hours later, I received Marlene's recorded message. These deliberately leaked facts traveled to Marlene with remarkable speed, and she responded in rapid measure.

Later I played Marlene's recorded message for my spy, keeping my wife's identity secret. On her next sleep-over with her boyfriend, she confronted her two-timing lover with the taped message and extracted an emotional confession.

Shortly thereafter, Marlene again gained entrance to PGA West and renewed surveillance of my home. I took action through the Security Chief, alerting neighbors, as well as Marlene's new consort. By the end of summer, she was once again *persona non grata* in our resort community.

My investigation of Marlene was complete, but how long would her threatening actions continue? The answer soon became clear. Long after the poisoning, I would look at my rear-view mirror and discover Everett tailing me. Marlene continued to besiege us through the mail and by phone. Some messages were disguised, but all had her unmistakable imprint:

"THE BEST REVENGE...WATCH OUT—STORMS AHEAD...OH EVIL ONE."

Marlene had often told me that she always had a hard time with the holidays, so it was not surprising that the harassment increased in late December 1995. Hang-up calls became more frequent, and one call was traced to her favorite video store. Marlene was identified as the customer using their counter phone at the exact time of the hang-up. At Christmas time, her newspaper ads betrayed her holiday loneliness and spotlighted current fantasies.

Marlene addressed a Christmas card to Mrs. Lucille Dunaway that contained a handwritten message for Lucille: "Keep the *faith—good* will surface over EVIL." Marlene was obviously mistaken about whom I had married.

It wasn't until about six months later she learned, via the double spy, that my wife was not Lucille. Marlene immediately wanted me to know this. Using a decorated envelope designed to catch a woman's eye, she fashioned a letter with diabolic innuendoes. She asked for the spurned diamond engagement ring I had given her in 1992, the one she had described as "a piece of crap." In the event I had given it to my wife, she wanted Ramona to know that I had purchased it for another woman. The Black Widow's final sting was her sign-off, "Your Ex-lover—Marlene."

The engagement ring was actually returned to the store years before, but I wasn't going to break the Restraining Order and give Marlene the satisfaction of a reply. Ramona and I couldn't help but laugh at her clumsy attempts to bring discord into the Dunaway household.

Throughout 1996, Marlene was still seeking sexual services from the polo trainer, and her voice-mail ads were still in the newspaper almost every week. Without Wallace Weller as a source of lucre, Marlene was now flying alone to Las Vegas on weekends. Her *modus operandi* remained the same, driven by a twisted psychopathic mind as dangerous as ever. Who would be next?

Unfortunately, she had not forgotten about me. Once Marlene discovered whom I had married, her interference became even more disruptive. She wrote letters to Ramona which claimed, for instance, that I had phoned her for sex. Both of us were relieved when Marlene's shenanigans appeared to cease early in 1997.

For a time, I wondered if Marlene had disappeared from the face of the desert. Then, six months after her last communication, Marlene's car was reported parked in an obscure spot near the offices of my investment firm. Was Marlene now employed by the company where all of my business and savings accounts were managed?

On August 12, 1997, I contacted my dependable broker. He didn't know Marlene, and did not realize she had been working in the offices since April under an alias. After several evidence-sharing sessions with him, he agreed she should be fired.

Much to my chagrin, I learned my broker had stepped down as Branch Manager, so the decision would have to be made by his replacement. When the new manager refused to see or speak to me, except to ask who won Marlene's suit for "BREACH OF PROMISE OF LANDLORD TO PAY FOR SEXUAL ENCOUNTERS," it became clear whom Marlene was currently "sexploiting" and why we hadn't heard from her for the past six months.

How terrifying to imagine her working in the office that managed my investments. Marlene knew very well that this firm handled my business, including her credit card account that I had canceled. She had passed her probationary period, thus was in a more trusted position.

After I wrote a steaming letter to the new branch manager about Marlene and her past actions, he suddenly transferred to the Las Vegas office. Following his reassignment, Marlene placed a new voice ad in the local newspaper. At the same time, she attempted to renew relationships with old and new flames in my gated community. Would the pictures of her and her sports car still posted at each gate ever slow her down?

When I pressured my investment firm for Marlene's dismissal, she sued me in Small Claims Court for sabotaging her job. Warren Stellar was pressed into service on my behalf and again reviewed the evidence against her. He suggested I list him as a possible witness.

"Marlene does not have a full deck," he warned me. "She is getting desperate." Fortunately, this must have been apparent to the judge, because she dismissed the suit and renewed the mutual Restraining Order for three years, 1998 to 2001. Nevertheless, the investment firm delayed terminating Marlene, citing fear of legal retaliation.

No matter. I quickly shifted my account to my former broker who had gone to another firm, taking his assistants with him. They confided suspicions that Marlene was tampering with their computers. Records showed she had accumulated over $100,000 by 1997 and had purchased her own home that year.

Marlene was finally dismissed at the same time her former lover was terminated from the Las Vegas branch office. She immediately applied for a position with my new investment company, not once, but twice. Representing herself with different names to two new brokers in that office, her bold ploy was discovered in-house before final interviews. Later

I was told she was blackballed by investment firms in the Palm Springs area. It had become clear she was still after me and my accounts.

After working as a broker's assistant, Marlene wasn't seen in public, at least by my crowd. Her voice ads were now dubbed by a girlfriend. When Marlene stalked me, as she did once in a boyfriend's golf cart, she wore her hair long and waved wildly at me with her outspread hand covering her face. She probably did not realize her hang-up calls were now recorded by my Caller ID, which I obtained as soon as it became available.

Seven years into my happy union with Ramona, and Marlene is still breaking the Restraining Order and harassing us, truly bent on revenge. To my friends this is unfathomable—until they remember that she is a psychopath.

"Marlene is a mirror-image of my sister," a friend of Ramona told me. "Having dealt with my sister's cunning nature, I can understand how easy it is to be fooled by a psychopath."

Optimistically, I sometimes hope she might distance herself or sink into anonymity. But according to all research on psychopathy, Marlene is at a point where she is unlikely to cease her actions. This vengeful woman still intends to exact a toll. Moreover, rumors had spread that Everett was part of the drug ring involved in the murder of his mother's former lover, Bernardo Gouthier.

*   *   *

As I sit in my study tonight, this millennium is closing. Leaning back in my chair, I watch our dog at play. Ramona's children rescued this puppy, a Border Collie/Labrador mix, when she was abandoned at a shopping center nearly ten years ago. She reminds me a lot of my Candy Dog—the same friendly brown eyes and lively personality. Ramona's dog is a trustworthy protector, giving me additional peace of mind at home.

I glance at a picture of my wife and reflect on the good times we have had together. Ramona is precious. Her warm smile and soft voice always make me feel comfortable.

As I contemplate what might have been, I am soothed even more. I know that without searching into Marlene's past, Ramona would not likely have entered my life. Now she is the centerpiece of my existence. A guardian angel must have been looking over me.

Ramona began as my interpreter, and her role is still the same: today she translates my waking days into an earthly paradise. Each morning as I rise beside her, I smile at the opportunity to spend time in her company.

The wonders of love! Ramona has made the separate parts of me whole, and in her I find new spiritual strength.

EPILOGUE

Initially, the reason for my investigation was to understand the truth behind the poisoning. Why did Marlene do it?

A new world of enlightenment was opened to me by research on Marlene's past. As her bizarre behavior pattern began to emerge and I learned more about psychopaths, my principal goal quickly shifted. It was more important to help others recognize and identify a "Marlene" in their own lives.

Had my relationship with Marlene spelled DOOMSDAY, it is unlikely that a homicide case would have been pursued by my family and friends. None would have ever cast Marlene as a murderess. The rational mind cannot easily understand the compelling forces that drive a psychopathic personality.

Crime experts attest that there have been hundreds of unsolved "perfect murders." Many are carried out so cleverly that they are written off as accidents; many are carried out by otherwise rational persons, capable of the most convoluted and elaborate of deceptions. Marlene is one of these individuals.

The medical profession admits that forensic science is often derelict when poisons are involved. "We don't ask ourselves whether an overdose can be attributable to attempted murder or not," a doctor told me. "We look at symptoms, and treat emergency situations." As a result, few quantitative toxicology tests are administered unless they are necessary to patient treatment or recovery. Moreover, few current non-fiction books go beyond the classic poisons and describe the potentially deadly drugs that are readily available by prescription or over-the-counter.

As nearly everyone will meet one or more psychopaths during their lifetime, it is important to know how dangerous they can be. They act like they are normal, but they are not!

Time sobers reflection, particularly now that I've had the opportunity to help identify other homicide suspects who are psychopaths. My close call at Marlene's hands sharpened my appreciation of what is truly important: LIFE, itself.

It is hoped this story opens the eyes of readers, and that it might help them avoid tragedy in their lives.

About the Author

▼

Brad Dunaway is a pseudonym for the author who prefers to remain anonymous in order to protect both himself and his family. The author has received acclaim with many books and articles published under his own name. He has recently published a well-received biography of a sports figure and is currently working on another.

www.ingramcontent.com/pod-product-compliance
Lightning Source LLC
Chambersburg PA
CBHW061246280526
45784CB00002B/652